BATTLE F

Battle for the Mind

DAVID HOLDEN

KINGSWAY PUBLICATIONS
EASTBOURNE

First published by Word UK for New Frontiers.
Published in 1998 by Kingsway Publications.
Reprinted with Study Guide in 1999.
This new edition 2001.

ISBN 1 84291 012 4

Published by
KINGSWAY PUBLICATIONS
Lottbridge Drove, Eastbourne, BN23 6NT, England.
Email: books@kingsway.co.uk

Book design and production for the publishers by
Bookprint Creative Services, P.O. Box 827, BN21 3YJ, England.
Printed in Great Britain.

I dedicate this book to everyone at Sidcup Community Church. I can never thank you enough for your constant love and support. Together we are looking to fulfil God's purposes for our lives as a people – and the best is yet to come!

Contents

Preface

How often do you hear the phrase, 'Oh, we tried that and it didn't work'? From reading a book on parenting to hearing a seminar on leadership skills, people seem to interpret what they hear as a 'quick fix' formula. Having returned home, they religiously copy the formula only to find that 'it doesn't work'! This can, of course, result in disillusionment and even guilt and condemnation.

I doubt that very much will happen unless you apply genuine and personal faith to what you hear and read. Your motivation to apply certain truths must never be driven by 'how to's' or formulas. If you approach *Battle for the Mind* in that way, you could easily fall into the category of, 'I tried that and it doesn't work'. This book is full of practical and hopefully helpful application, but it's not a quick fix solution, or a manual of rules promising success.

Grace is the touchstone. We have been saved by grace – something entirely undeserved – and we must depend on grace in every area of life, including the renewing of our minds. You may be reading this book and making great progress in mind renewal. But suppose you suddenly fail. Do you think, 'I'll never keep going so I may as well give up'? No. You remind yourself that formulas will never enable you to press on. You need grace. Grace never brings you to the point of saying, 'I tried that and it didn't work.' It says, 'I'll help you to get through.' This book may encourage you, but don't let it govern your life. Receive God's grace and work with God as He brings renewal to your mind.

Well over a decade has passed since this book was first published. I have been amazed at how many times people have come to me and thanked me for its practical application either to them personally, as they have gone through the material with a new believer, or as they have used it in small group studies. Since then this book has been revised and updated to become more relevant to us as Christians as our society changes. I am very much aware that I am still working through the content of the book on a daily basis. The material is perhaps more relevant to the many folk in our churches who have become Christians since it was first written. I trust that it will enable many whose minds have been damaged by wrong thinking to be genuinely transformed through the renewing of their minds.

Introduction

Defeated by temptation? Lack of growth and fruitfulness? Most of your problems are in your mind.

You are still thinking the old way. You have been born again by the Spirit of God, but nothing much has happened in your mind. The potential that you have to overcome the lies of the enemy and to live a victorious life remains just potential.

Are you still dominated by fears from the past? Do you suffer anxiety? Do you find that you cannot shake off self-pity or a sense of rejection? Are you still tyrannised by lustful thoughts? A sorry state! What is worse, it can go on for years!

This problem is not simply associated with young people or young Christians; it is amazingly widespread. Some Christians live their lives in a state of permanent defeat. How sad when it need not be so.

We are surrounded by pressures which, if succumbed to, influence our minds and our thinking in ungodly ways. Sometimes subtly, sometimes more directly, many people use the powerful communication ability of the media to put their priorities and their message across and to influence our minds away from God.

Our background and our upbringing, our friends at school and our favourite teachers all influenced us in the past. The question is: what is the dominant influence on your mind today as a Christian?

This book aims to take hold of the defeated mind and the easily diverted mind and help you begin to reach out for all the potential that is yours in Christ and make it your own.

This is an exciting and very radical opportunity. The power of God which is at work within you can change your thinking!

Even more radical is the possibility that, having begun along this road of renewal of the mind, you will be increasingly equipped to help others.

Now that's something else!

PART ONE

Why Renew Your Mind?

1. How Vital Is the Renewed Mind?

Our aim: The Word of God is absolutely clear: it is vital that as Christians we change the way we think. The Bible says it is essential if we are to live victorious Christian lives. We should be in no doubt about the vital role our minds have in shaping us as people.

Let us take one particular verse as an example: 'as he thinks within himself, so he is' (Prov 23:7, NASB). To reinforce the message, let us rewrite it in its most basic form so that we get the full impact of it: 'As you think, so you are.' That is why it is so vital for your mind to be renewed. It is what is floating around in your mind which will affect the way you behave on a daily basis.

The way you think affects your attitudes, your hopes and your fears. The way you think affects the way you react to people, the way you speak to others, and how you handle your job and its pressures. It affects the way you raise your family if you are a parent, and the way you relate to your own father and mother, and the way you handle being part of the growing single population in our society today.

You will probably be able to remember a couple of examples from your own experience where your thinking caused problems for you when it slipped out in your speech or in your actions. Thoughts always end up affecting our actions. You can think something and sooner or later it will infiltrate your behaviour. That influence can be for good or it can be for bad, depending on the way you think. The way you act depends on the way you think.

Here is a typical example for single young men. One day, you meet a gorgeous girl. A thought comes into your mind along the lines of: 'Wow! How tremendous!' You've started something and it can end up in a walk down the aisle! You have to be careful with thoughts.

When I met my wife for the first time, the first thought that came into my mind was, 'Terrific!' I tried to rebuke it, but it wouldn't go away. It was a good thought, a nice thought, and it led to action.

Conversely, it can work the other way. Here is an example from my schooldays. I am standing in Woolworths on the way home from school. No one is particularly looking at what I'm doing and there are the rows of sweets arranged along the counter in front of me. The thought comes, just a little thought: 'Go on, do it.' I used to have a black gabardine raincoat with huge pockets in it, just to increase the temptation. The tragedy of people hooked on shoplifting is that it all started one day just like that: the little thought became an action.

Remember the little catch phrase, 'I did it without thinking', beloved of schoolchildren – and others! Think through the sequence of events carefully – is it really 'without thinking'?

Consider even habitual actions. There is always a thought, even a very spontaneous and quick one, before the action is undertaken. The mind has to say to the body, 'Move!' There's a temptation, then there's a thought, and then the action comes.

It is vital to renew the mind. As Christians we must take control of our actions. Therefore, we need to take control of our minds. Our minds have to know how to deal with the daily barrage of thoughts if we are to overcome sin.

The process

Let us look at a key verse for the subject of the mind: 'Do not conform any longer to the pattern of this world, but be transformed by the renewing of your mind' (Rom 12:2).

The word used in the Greek for 'transformed' is the same word which forms the root of our word 'metamorphosis'. It is the same word as Paul uses in 2 Corinthians 3:18 where he speaks about us being transformed into the likeness of Christ with ever-increasing glory.

We're not just to be affected or influenced by our Christian faith; we're to see a revolution occur in our thinking.

If you like you could rephrase Romans 12:2 to say something like, 'Be transformed, be rearranged, be totally changed, be completely and utterly removed and moved on.'

The process is gradual

The Bible says some dramatic things about what happens when we become Christians. For most of us it takes some time to grasp all that God has done in that rebirth, because such a lot happens without us fully realising it at first. Here are just some of the truths about your rebirth:

- 'He has rescued us from the dominion of darkness and brought us into the kingdom of the Son he loves' (Col 1:13).
- 'The old has gone, the new has come!' (2 Cor 5:17).
- 'All . . . are justified freely by his grace through the redemption that came by Christ Jesus' (Rom 3:24).
- 'To all who received him, to those who believed in his name, he gave the right to become children of God' (Jn 1:12).
- 'If anyone is in Christ, he is a new creation' (2 Cor 5:17).

The Bible says that when you receive a new heart, you receive a new spirit, a new nature. You have a new song in your heart and on your lips, but nowhere do the Scriptures say you receive a new mind.

Romans 12:2 says 'Be transformed by the renewing of . . .' not 'by renewing'. It says that you are to renew your mind. The implication is that the old mind you used to have is still there! Some of us might feel a little disappointed with that; perhaps we were hoping for a new mind with about twice as much IQ! What a shame!

This is a vital lesson to learn: a new mind didn't just drop out of heaven. We didn't wake up on the first day of our new Christian life with a mind that had been replaced in the night. We soon discover that instant holiness and instant righteous thinking is not how it is.

The good news is that it's the same old mind, but the *process of change* can begin. It's going to be changed, it's going to be renewed, it's going to be transformed. For most of us that process can certainly be quicker than it is, but it is still a process.

The process is from the world

A transformation involves two extremes, two sides: what we are transformed from, and what we are transformed into.

The renewing of our mind will transform us from the pattern of this world (Rom 12:2). This is radical! Sadly, many Christians, when they are first born again, are placed under a very legalistic way of living. The intentions are good and honourable – to help them develop Christian character – but the result is usually ineffective. This is because they only deal with the outward appearance and not with the mind.

Legalism has nothing to do with the way you think, but rather the way you dress, the way you behave, the sort of films, television and music which is 'acceptable', and the achievement of goals in terms of meetings attended, chapters of the Bible read, etc.

Of course the way you dress will reflect your background, the way you are and the way you think. For example, people can adopt a distinctive style of dress out of a spirit of rebellion. Something within rebels and it affects the way they dress. Later it becomes fashionable.

When someone like that is saved the idea is not that he or she conforms to the way Christians dress, but rather to the way Christians think. As that transformation in the mind away from the world's thinking occurs, it will probably affect the way that person dresses. You will see an outworking of a changed mind. We don't impose a law on dress, but changed dress will be the fruit which we will later see from a changed mind. Much of modern day fashion is driven by sex and a great deal of advertising reflects this. If a person becomes a Christian and their mind is being renewed, their views on sex will change, and this will cause them to think about the way they dress. (Parents of teenagers would do well to talk about these issues openly.)

Review

This is so important and fundamental a concept for the renewing of your mind that you should stop here and review it. Have you grasped the difference between the outward 'law' and the inward working of grace on your mind?

The process is to link you into God's purposes

The second phrase of Romans 12:2 says: 'Then you will be able to test and approve what God's will is – his good, pleasing and perfect will.'

Guidance is another area where Christians seem to struggle. We can be very woolly over guidance, and there are Christians around who still resort to sticking pins onto the pages of their Bible.

Here is a *key* to guidance. The reason many of us struggle

with guidance is that we haven't been renewed in the way that we think. Our minds are cluttered up with all sorts of other thoughts and jargon, what other people think and how they will react, so that we cannot discern the direction God is leading us, and what He is saying.

As our minds are renewed and transformed into godly ways of thinking and looking at situations, we will discover that they are more settled and more confident. In that context the way we live will be increasingly clear and decisions will have less uncertainty to them. There will still be calls to steps of faith, but we will know more clearly that those steps are the call of God. Guidance is actually quite simple. Jesus said, 'My sheep hear my voice.'

Is your mind uncontrolled?

Many Christians are dominated by their sin 'problems': their habits, their behaviour, their appearance, etc. They are trying to change their 'self' without ever dealing with the root problem, which is the way we think. So change the way you think and you will begin to deal with the sin problems that remain in your life.

God's ultimate purpose is for us all to become like Jesus. That's not just a glib phrase to be looked at and acknowledged. We have got to start thinking the way He thinks. When we begin to think about issues the way Jesus does, we know we are becoming more like Him. If you are to be changed to be like Jesus, you must first begin to think like Him in order that, as a result, your character and actions might be reflective of Him.

For that to begin to happen we need controlled minds. Is your mind under control?

Here are some examples of the uncontrolled mind at work.

Stress and anxiety

Some doctors estimate that as many as 70 per cent of their waiting-room patients may have a physical problem that is actually a product of their mind and their thoughts. The mind is a powerful instrument.

For example, the Jones family have the flu and you visit them. A little thought comes in: 'If I visit them I might catch it.' By the time you're on the doorstep ringing the bell your legs ache,your back aches and you feel all hot and sweaty.

Take another example: a stressful thought can have repercussions that are physical. An anxious thought can lead to illness. People suffer like that, even Christians, because their minds are uncontrolled. Hypnosis is increasingly recognised as a means of therapy for anxiety and stress. Needless to say, this is hardly a wholesome means of controlling your mind – in fact it's the opposite.

Now by no means all fearful and anxious thoughts will result in such conditions, but it illustrates the devastation an uncontrolled mind can reap. And anyway, who wants to be in the grip of fear and anxiety?

Sexual temptation

With David and Bathsheba (2 Sam 11) sin didn't begin with an action. It began with a thought. In fact, it began with a thought in an ill-disciplined mind. David should have been leading his troops on the battlefield, his adrenaline surging and his mind razor-sharp. Instead he was wandering around his palace, dissipating his time in idle thoughts and idle behaviour. In that environment he was very vulnerable. The sight of a beautiful woman sent his thought life pounding down uncontrolled tracks.

Lust is a massive problem for a lot of people, and not just among the men either. That whole area of lust, pornography, fantasy and sexual bombardment from the world gains its entry via our thinking. That is where the attack is concentrated – in your mind. Accessibility to sexual temptation has never been greater than it is today. It increasingly penetrates our home life via TV (especially cable and satellite) and now computers can provide us with instant temptation via the Internet. This is not a game. It is real and ruins lives every day.

Cynicism

Here is another big one for us, especially the British. We are a cynical race of people. It's certainly something most British Christians need to be transformed from. We are brought up in a cynical way of thinking through school and this is continually reinforced through television and the media generally throughout our adult lives. This is an enormous barrier to Christian thinking – it affects the way we think, the way we analyse situations and the way we respond to others.

Cynicism can be devastating to our speech and personality. It starts in the mind, and can run uncontrolled.

Negativism

Perhaps related to cynicism, negativism is such a large part of many Christians' background. It can be really damaging. Parents can speak persistently negative things to their children and it takes root in their thinking. Maybe you were always bottom or almost bottom of the class, and even as an adult you have never been encouraged in your abilities. What happens over the years is that you develop a habitually negative way of thinking, especially about yourself.

Self-pity

Low self-image can lead to frequent pity-parties. The truth is that God has never said anything to make you feel self-pity or to have a low self-image. Actually, He does the opposite, so where on earth did this way of thinking come from? An unrenewed mind! It is contrary to the Word of God, so we need to deal with it. It never ceases to amaze me how easily Christians can give in to a false view of themselves, and yet at the same time struggle so much with how God sees them. Who is right? It's time to change our thinking.

Anger

Some people have enormous problems when it comes to anger. It begins in the way you think. Many people manage to hold their anger within their thoughts. In that way they control their actions, and they don't retaliate verbally or physically, but the thought is there. Big and ugly.

For some it does occasionally spill over into verbal abuse

and even physical reaction, but it still starts the same way – in an uncontrolled mind.

Fears

Some people have fears that are based on traumatic experiences of the past, but the uncontrolled mind has allowed that trauma to run riot, to walk all over their everyday experience.

Imagine the typical scene: a child of four or five years old is walking along the road and a great, enormous dog comes bounding up, all bright-eyed and full of fun. The tail swishes, the dog barks and the child is terrified of this overwhelming animal. A moment in time, a fearsome thought and it's the beginning of a lifelong fear of dogs that affects that person's behaviour and personality.

The good news is that the effect of that trauma on our minds and actions can be erased as our minds are renewed in Christ. So many people have fears in their lives. Whatever the root, be it something which happened in the past or even fear of the future, in my experience it is the most frequently mentioned battle area of the mind. I have come to believe that it is Satan's greatest ploy to trigger a series of other harmful thoughts. Fear is his entry point. Once we learn to deal with fear then his activity is seriously thwarted. The details of how to actually deal with fear through the renewing of the mind will be covered in Part Two of this book, but for now you need to know that you are not alone in your fears.

If Satan can cause you to fear, you have fallen into one of his schemes. Over the years I have often woken suddenly in the night – no doubt due to disturbed dreaming, or being over-tired, or perhaps just plain indigestion. I'm sure there are probably rational explanations for this. However, I have been amazed at how often I find my mind to be full of fearful thoughts during these unwelcome awakenings and occasionally even an awareness of fear 'in the room'.

Handling that fear is the issue, not what may follow on afterwards, and Christians must simply get to grips with the whole concept of fear otherwise we may find ourselves an easy target for enemy thought patterns. Fear has been dealt with on the cross. When Jesus rose from the dead, even our last enemy death was gloriously defeated. Even the fear of death itself was dealt with in that moment.

Hebrews 2:15 states, '. . . and free those who all their lives were held in slavery by their fear of death.'

Fear can dominate your mind – it's in the mind therefore that you can deal with fear. Why not even now begin to fill your mind with this thought – 'There is no fear in love. But perfect love drives out fear' (1 Jn 4:18)?

Renewing the mind is absolutely vital for every Christian, however much or little you have been able to identify yourself with those examples given above. It is essential because it will affect our whole lifestyle and our ability to walk in the ways God has prepared for us for His glory.

2. The State of Your Mind

In this chapter we will be looking at the two states of mind: first, before you were in Christ, and, secondly, now you are in Christ. Finally, we will explore the dynamics of the change from one state to the other.

1. Before you were in Christ

Romans 1 is a chapter all about men and women away from Christ. Men and women, born in Adam, have an inclination towards belief and an awareness that, out there, there is a living God, yet they have turned away from God and have attempted to live by their own knowledge and power.

Romans 1:28 says, 'Since they did not think it worth while to retain the knowledge of God, he gave them over to a depraved mind, to do what ought not to be done.' The phrase 'gave them over' appears again in verses 24, 26 and 28.

God made His judgement on the way they were thinking,

on the way their minds were working. He said in effect, 'OK. Enough is enough. I give you over. Have your own way then and reap its fruit.' So then, before we were in Christ our minds were depraved, bent towards thinking improper, unclean and self-destroying thoughts. Our minds were full of sin.

It is, for those outside of Christ, a natural process. You do not have to train children to argue. You do not have to teach little brothers and sisters to fight over toys. They do it naturally. Naughtiness comes with an amazing sense of ease and ability. They seem made for it!

Ephesians 2:3 tells us that before we were in Christ we gratified the cravings of our sinful nature and followed its desires and thoughts. See how important it is that we understand this. It doesn't matter what sort of home you were brought up in. You may have been brought up in a Christian home, your dad may even have been an elder. Or you may not have known who your parents were. That is all irrelevant. By nature, by your very being on this planet, you would naturally indulge the desires of your mind.

Before we were in Christ we were darkened in our understanding and separated from the life of God. Our hearts were hardened (Eph 4:17,18).

To give you an example, over the years I've been in many situations witnessing to folk who, outwardly at least, appear to be very 'spiritually minded'. They are perhaps into New Age philosophy or some kind of 'peace movement', or have strong views on the environment, etc. The conversation can be going well until we mention Jesus. Suddenly these peaceful, 'spiritually aware' people become remarkably violent in their verbal reaction. We just talked about Jesus and suddenly peace was gone. They may have been proclaiming their hopes for a better spiritual future, but their hearts were hardened to the claims of Jesus that real peace only comes through Him. The reaction of hardening rebellious hearts was there all along – our conversation just exposed it.

Colossians 1:21 tells us that we were once alienated from God and enemies in our minds. We don't like this. It's not comfortable. But the Bible is clear that before we were in Christ our minds were darkened and our thinking was futile. There is a sense in which we were kept away from God – alienated and enemies – because of our thinking. You will see the same idea expressed in 2 Corinthians 4:3.

Before you were in Christ Satan hung a veil over your thinking, distorting and denying the truth of God. He blinded you from seeing things as you ought to see them.

Nevertheless ...

Romans 1 reminds us that even looking at creation alone it is plain to see that there is a God. The 'argument from design' (as it is known) is a very powerful one. Colleges and universities are full of people doing philosophy and similar subjects because deep inside all of us there is this half-acknowledged cry that there must be a God. Go to any campus and you'll find students earnestly discussing the origin of things. Most, the more honest anyway, would admit it takes a very big leap of faith indeed to believe it all just came about by chance.

Titus 1:15 tells us that the minds and consciences of unbelievers are corrupted. The Bible is very clear that you have a conscience too. Not only can I discover God in creation, but

I can see Him reflected in my conscience. I knew what was right and wrong before I was a Christian. Didn't you?

In the sixties and seventies we were taught that free living and casual sex were all right. This was really a corrupted conscience battling against itself, proclaiming loudly to drown out the conviction that actually the truth was otherwise. By the nineties we were living in the consequences of so-called permissiveness and observing its devastating effects upon a new generation. A generation without any semblance of biblical morality in its thinking.

Before you were in Christ you had a conscience. It was there – bent, corrupted, defiled, weak, easily conned and twisted – but still there. Many people are easily led and allow their consciences to be easily overrun.

For example, there is a growing pressure these days for young people, at an ever increasingly younger age, to analyse their sexuality. The question 'Am I gay or am I straight?' is now clearly spoken about, even in some cases, pre-teens. The problem is, of course, that an already defiled conscience is in great danger of being forced into answering that question wrongly. Even the question itself is suggestive, and one has to wonder how many gay men, for example, have adopted a gay lifestyle not through freedom of choice, but through peer pressure. Can a fourteen-year-old really know his or her emotional response to such issues?

I believe a lot of people get into things they never really assented to. They never had any intention of touching these things, but because a process of thinking got hold of them, and their minds were uncontrolled and their consciences darkened, they were unable to resist.

Have you ever wondered why people seem so incapable sometimes of understanding the gospel? It's so simple, yet they seem as thick as two planks! I sat through gospel service after gospel service, rebellious and angry. Surprise, surprise! I didn't understand any of it. It was alien to me because my mind was veiled to the truth. I remained alienated and far from God with my mind the playground of God's enemy, Satan.

You may say that you were a pretty decent sort of person before you were a Christian. The problem is God doesn't just look at the actions, He looks at the *thoughts* of a man too. Jesus said that even to look on a woman in an adulterous way is to commit adultery. Just the thought is enough. God sees our motives and our thoughts, and we are full of sin, through and through.

2. Now you are in Christ

Something tremendously exciting happens when you are born again. God lifts the veil. For the first time in your life the light of God begins to penetrate your darkened mind. The veil over your understanding is lifted. It's as if the gateway to your mind is swung open by the Lord Himself and He steps inside.

Suddenly, you understand things. Scripture verses spring to life, the songs in the meetings take on a meaning you'd missed before and you know heaven has invaded your thinking. In Hebrews 10:16 God promises that He will put His laws in our hearts and write them on our minds. And in Hebrews 10:22 we read that we can have 'our hearts sprinkled to cleanse us from a guilty conscience'.

As your mind begins to understand truth and you learn to live in it, it will set you free. Your conscience can remain clean, it can be brought alive, made acute and powerful again.

You may have heard truth before, but it was ineffective and your mind was full of lies. Now that you are in Christ, speaking truth to yourself will be effective. It will train you, it will formulate your thinking and it will set you free. Wonderful gospel! How exciting! It will actually affect your life!

Hebrews tells us that, under the old covenant, the blood of bulls and goats could never actually erase sin. It was a symbolic act. The people would watch the goats going off into the wilderness and they would know that symbol of death to sin would mean their forgiveness for another year.

The problem was that it never actually got into the bloodstream, it never penetrated their minds to chase away evil in their thinking; it never touched their hearts or their consciences.

But Hebrews says of Jesus that His blood has touched our hearts and our consciences. It means my sin has actually been dealt with for ever, and that in my innermost being are springs of living water which can reach right into my mind to renew it and transform me.

You can have a renewed mind, you can have your impure thoughts, wrong motives, jealousies and fears dealt with by the Lord. This work of Jesus is all-powerful and able to deal with the enemy in all areas of your life – including and especially in your mind.

That has happened to you in Christ: light has invaded darkness, truth has invaded lies, your conscience has become acute and the veil has been removed to reveal understanding.

This is the state of your mind in Christ.

3. The dynamics of change

The crunch is this: it is not an instant process. That is not a depressing notion, but a releasing one for us. So many Christians live in a state of guilt about their minds based on this error. They believe their minds should have been instantly changed; they're some sort of second-rate, unholy Christian.

Understand this vital message: renewing the mind is a process of change.

Destroying domination from the past

Many Christians are truly confused when they discover that despite being born again, baptised in water, baptised in the Spirit and all the other wonderful things of the kingdom of God, they are still bugged by that same fear, phobia or problem that's been with them for years.

Have you noticed? You still have problems. God doesn't whisk you away from potentially fearful situations if you have a problem or fear. You don't discover endless daylight after you're saved if your problem is fear of the dark.

The Lord wants to teach you how to handle these situations with a renewed mind. When that is learned there is a real and permanent victory for the gospel.

Taking every thought captive

We often come across Christians who have deep-seated problems from the past still reaching forward into their experiences today. Sometimes these people need deliverance ministry. Such ministry can be very effective and very powerful in destroying the unwarranted clutches of the devil on a person's life. However, our experience is often that, sadly, this sort of person falls back into similar difficulties.

What is the answer? More deliverance ministry? Was the first ministry unsuccessful then? No. We believe passionately that Jesus died to set the captive free, and He does. A person can be liberated in a moment, but what is necessary to *stay* free is a *renewed mind*. If a person learns to think according to the Word of God then that will enable them to stay clear and build fresh godly ways where before they were open to the enemy re-dominating their mind. It follows, therefore, that any kind of deliverance that a Christian may face must be accompanied by good teaching on how to renew their minds or they will only struggle and even fall back again.

Review

So, before we were in Christ, our minds were thinking futile thoughts, enemies of God, distorted in conscience and full of sin. Now, in Christ we are totally forgiven, our conscience is liberated and we are being flooded with understanding and truth. A process of change has begun. It's a learning process, tapping into that new life within to bring about a renewing of our minds. What a great adventure lies ahead!

3. Who Do You Think You Are?

Before we get into the battle for the mind, that dynamic process of change which is open to you now you are saved, it is necessary to draw together all that we have touched on in the first two chapters about our background and what we are being renewed from. Let us nail some issues. Use this chapter to bring clarity, not condemnation!

The effect of our upbringing

A major part of our background is, of course, how we were brought up. Proverbs 22:6 says, 'Train a child in the way he should go, and when he is old he will not turn from it.' This is the Word of God to parents and, as Christians, we want to work that through with our own children.

Unfortunately, it is also true that if you have been trained in bad ways as a child, in wrong thinking and critical attitudes, you will find those ways as difficult to shake off as the areas you were well trained in. It is much easier to stay with something you're used to rather than face up to a whole new way of thinking.

Independence

A girl who became a Christian a few years ago had had a very difficult upbringing. Her father had died when she was ten. Her mother sat the children together after the funeral and asked them if they felt hurt.

'Yes,' they all said, 'it hurts a lot because Daddy has gone.'

'Right,' Mum replied, 'and I am going to bring you up never to get close to anyone ever again so that you never have the possibility of facing this hurt again.'

So she was brought up that way: never expressing herself emotionally, never letting herself get close or open up to anyone. She lived an isolated life, just considering herself. When she was born again and entered the kingdom of God it was wonderful. Gloriously baptised in the Spirit and set free, she went on tremendously for a few months.

Then the background began to reassert itself. Her background began to clash with the Word of God. Nowhere in the Word do you find God saying, 'Be independent, live for yourself.' In fact God says the very opposite – love one another, consider one another, open up your life to one another.

The way she got through was that she started to allow the Word of God to dominate her thinking. It was difficult at first and it took time, but gradually her ways were transformed by the renewing of her mind.

She had built walls round her life, but became a Christian and God smashed down the walls. Suddenly, she could see the horizon again! But her background reasserted itself: she felt exposed and in a dangerous place, so she started to rebuild the walls almost automatically. To stop and reverse that process she had to take the Word of God to her mind so that her past ceased to dominate her present.

Parental domination

Here is an area which often causes difficulties. Not least because the Word of God is clear that we should obey our parents as children and continue to honour them when we ourselves are in adulthood.

Often, however, we come across Christians who are under undue domination by their parents. This is a situation which can dominate, even as adults and even with Christian parents. Inevitably, there will be clashes with the kingdom of God.

Jesus said, 'Anyone who loves his father or mother more than me is not worthy of me; anyone who loves his son or daughter more than me is not worthy of me' (Matt 10:37). In other words, He should come first in our lives. This is difficult for us. Just before Jesus said these words He declared, 'I did not come to bring peace, but a sword' (Matt 10:34). We find that the sword is a painful thing sometimes. Yet it is to the end that we are free in our thinking and free to have a right and wholesome relationship with our parents.

Jesus Himself had to face this very issue when enormous emotional pressure came to bear upon Him from His family. We read: 'Then Jesus' mother and brothers arrived. Standing outside, they sent someone in to call him. A crowd was sitting around him, and they told him, "Your mother and brothers are outside looking for you." "Who are my mother and my brothers?" he asked. Then he looked at those seated in a circle around him and said, "Here are my mother and my brothers! Whoever does God's will is my brother and sister and mother"' (Mk 3:31–34). Jesus discovered that this 'domination' was directly aimed at preventing Him fulfilling His ministry. How many Christians fail to fulfil their destiny due to a compromise with family pressure? Is that you?

Parental expectations

Another area of difficulty some of us have suffered is the persistent sense of failing to do as well as expected.

'Well, not bad, but . . .!'

'Second, huh! Well, you had it in you to come first, you know.'

This is how teenagers find themselves hitting the Valium to survive 'A' levels – striving all the time to achieve, while inside they are dying through lack of love, support and compassion.

It needs to be rooted out of the mind. It is alien to the love and grace of God, and it is contrary to His attitude towards you.

Negativism

This, too, is often born out of bad attitudes from parents which are persistently drummed into us.

'You're useless, you're hopeless, you're as bad as your father!'

Sadly, so often we hear of upbringing where phrases like that rang round someone's mind year in, year out. It's devastating, and such an upbringing will continue to dominate your life until you let the truth of God's Word win the battle and reorientate your self-esteem.

Traumas

Sometimes you will discover people who have suffered dramatic or devastating events in their life which have dominated their response in certain situations. The memory keeps reverberating around their minds.

For example, many suffered traumatically as children in the war, and have abiding memories which seem somehow to carry their sting even into the new life in the kingdom of God.

We could quote many other examples of trauma, particularly in childhood, but the point is this: God can heal you of the impact of those things on your life, and your mind can be renewed so that your character is transformed into one unaffected by those events. It simply does not matter how great the trauma and its effects have been upon you – your mind can be renewed.

Present-day pressures

The world in which we live is constantly trying to mould us into its way of thinking. There is daily pressure to be conformed to its attitudes and values. Just as we need to be renewed from our upbringing, so we need to be renewed from these unhealthy values which we have absorbed from the world. These things, too, become part of our background.

Materialism

Most Christians get into difficulties not because they have a lot of money to spend, but because of the way they think and their attitudes towards wealth. We could all use a lot more money if we had it, couldn't we? The issue is attitude, and attitudes reside in the mind.

The verse in the Bible most misquoted (by the world) is 1 Timothy 6:10. It doesn't say that *money* is a root of all kinds of evil; it says that it is the *love of money* that causes the problem. Materialism isn't a question of how much money you have, but a question of attitude. You can actually have hardly anything and still have problems of attitude. In fact, you can be quite poor yet be very materialistic in your outlook.

The Bible is radical, isn't it! Jesus said: 'You cannot serve both God and Money' (Matt 6:24). The idea is that we serve the Lord and we receive whatever He provides. But if we don't live for money, we aren't motivated in our thinking and therefore in our decision-making by the priorities of gaining wealth.

It's interesting how twisted and self-deceiving the world can be on this subject. Look at your newspaper with the gossip columns and news often gloating over the unhappiness and mess of the lives of the rich. Turn the page and see the promotional offers: win this, win that, be happy! Does winning the lottery fulfil you? Not according to many who have won it.

Permissiveness

How easy it is to absorb the world's values in this area. Are Christians simply following along behind at a discreet distance?

Many of us have been duped by sophisticated permissiveness on our televisions. Soaps, for example, present us with 'how it is' out there. Does that make it acceptable? What life values are being presented to you? It may be sophisticated, it may not be explicit, but what is the philosophy you are absorbing as you watch? Try this test: leave it for a year and then switch on again. It's just a different bed and a different couple, but the same story line.

What about the 'realistic' soaps? The nitty-gritty of life in all its raw-edged detail. Bombarding you with 'realism', but with what sort of flavour? Do you need to be 'entertained' by lives portraying the mess of a godless society? 'But it's a reflection of real life,' people say – but is it? So many soaps portray one side of adultery, for example, yet fail to show you the heartache of innocent parties affected by it. That's real!

These are the attitudes that dominate our society today. They are a time bomb eroding everything, but especially the security and happiness of godly family life. As Christians we can still be letting our minds absorb some of these values almost without noticing or caring until we discover that we've lost out in the battle for the mind.

Passivity

This is becoming an increasing problem for us to face as Christians. It is probably one of those national characteristics like cynicism which so easily invade our lives. In these days of progressive feminism it is particularly a problem for men.

We cop out, we back off, we try to stay as uninvolved as possible. It's a sort of defence mechanism. It's illustrated in the increasing portrayal of men in television comedy as wet wimps, dominated by the women in the story line. Perhaps you've noticed it's not just vicars who get this treatment these days!

It can saturate men's attitudes. We wile away the hours, we wile away the years and life goes by as we dissipate ourselves, leaving the radical edge, the achievement in life, the goal-getting to others.

If that has even begun to enter your thinking, you need to be liberated and to have your mind renewed. Such is the modern-day confusion of this issue that Christians have now even entered the debate on 'What is masculinity and what is femininity?' It is good to do this, but let us not fall into the same trap as the world – a 'sea of confusion' – which we will do, unless we tackle it biblically and not just culturally. It's wonderful that more and more women are feeling greater freedom to express their femininity, but men increasingly need help to understand their masculinity as well. The way we think is crucial in all of this.

Fearfulness

Just as this can be a pressure from our upbringing so also it can be a pressure for us if we allow society's fears to infiltrate our Christian security in God.

People in our society today have an almost Pavlovian reaction to the news. Any disaster anywhere in the world will enter their thinking and dominate them with fear for their own future. You can list a few very easily by listening and observing: fear of war in the Middle East and its consequences, of sickness epidemics, of contaminated food, of the greenhouse effect, or train crashes and bombs on aircraft – a world full of fear.

Some Christians allow themselves to live in fears like that, indistinguishable from the unregenerate who indeed has 'no hope and is without God in the world'. We need the truth of God to renew our minds, to liberate our thinking into the security He brings.

Media pressures

For most people the media have the function of doing their thinking for them. This is especially true of television. You switch off mentally, they switch on – feeding you, instructing you, training you, convincing you. If your mind is not renewed you absorb the whole lot – hook, line and sinker. And you're sunk!

Of course the great cry of the opponents of Christianity is that you are moulded, you become narrow in your thinking. We need to refute that utterly. The reverse is true because the *media* are the greatest opportunity the world has for moulding attitudes, ideas and thinking. They have entry to your mind, and their philosophy – up front or subtly behind the scenes – is humanism in various forms.

Not so long ago presenting homosexuality as a valid alternative lifestyle in schools was considered by an overwhelming majority of teachers to be wrong. Today the story is totally different. Have the issues changed? No? Then who has changed their minds? Opinion makers have won a battle for people's attitudes.

We need to be continually renewed from the pressures of the media. Adverts decide what's good-looking, what's in fashion; television decides ethics and feeds the theories of a godless, evolutionary society in its documentaries. Political correctness is a very strong 'pressure issue' these days. One wonders how much time is spent by the media ensuring that the product being sold is packaged in acceptable terms. Whether political correctness is going overboard or actually necessary is not the issue here; rather it is a classic example of the need to conform. The media do that all the time and people just go along with it. It is difficult to stand up against the crowd. Peer pressure is more evident today than at any time before. But what if it is wrong and contradicts the way we should think as Christians?

We need to be renewed in our minds by the truth of God to stand clear on His principles while still remaining firmly part of our society. We don't want to be ascetics, withdrawing from contact with the world, but rather we want our lives to count as a proclamation of the kingdom of God. If that means being different, then so be it.

Culture

One area where we may well find ourselves to be different is in a potential clash with modern culture. I have always been one to desire that the Christian church be culturally relevant and I often cringe where Christianity is portrayed in strange and perhaps archaic forms quite irrelevant to those we're endeavouring to communicate with. We ought to be relevant, culturally informed, and creative in how we communicate Jesus to a modern secularised society. However, I have to come to terms with the fact that much of what I believe and practise is at odds with modern culture and that the gospel is and always will be above culture rather than submitted to it. Certainly in our day the gospel is considered and then rejected by our culture.

Christians should not be culturally cloned! Or as Paul put it 'Do not conform any longer to the pattern [way of thinking: culture] of this world' (Rom 12:2). A growing pressure in Western Christianity is indeed to conform to our culture, often with the most genuine of intentions, e.g. to be relevant. It has to be said, however, that where our culture clashes with God's declared will, e.g. sex outside of marriage, it is not culture that should dominate our thinking, but God's Word. To refuse to yield to cultural pressure may result in all kinds of misunderstanding, not to mention direct opposition, but seeing things the way God sees them will be of eternal value. After all, cultures (like fashion) come and go. God's Word remains for ever.

PART TWO

The Battleground

4. Taking Every Thought Captive

Now that we are convinced that renewing the mind is vital, we can press on to see how the Lord wants us to go about it. We have looked at the issues where our minds need to be renewed, and we can appreciate how impoverished our Christian life will be if there is no change in the area of our thinking.

We are going to look at the battleground and see that we have been provided with suitable weapons. Using these weapons your life can be changed. We can become men and women who are victorious in the kingdom of God.

Take every thought captive

Paul tells the Corinthians, 'I beg you that when I come I may not have to be as bold as I expect to be towards some people who think that we live by the standards of this world. For though we live in the world, we do not wage war as the world does. The weapons we fight with are not the weapons of the world. On the contrary, they have divine power to demolish strongholds. We demolish arguments and every pretension that sets itself up against the knowledge of God, and we take captive every thought to make it obedient to Christ' (2 Cor 10:2–5).

When the Bible talks about strongholds, it is referring to the strongholds of the enemy. Until you were in Christ your mind was actually the territory of Satan and he ruled and reigned there whether you were aware of it or not. In fact he had such a field day there he built strongholds to consolidate his position.

Now that you have been born again Christ has authority, and far greater authority. You have been delivered from the kingdom of darkness and the rule of Satan into the kingdom of God, where Jesus rules. There is authority there to pull down and destroy everything that Satan has built up over the years. Jesus has final authority in your life.

What you have to realise is that Satan doesn't want to give up without a fight. There is a battle on. He has dominated your thinking and driven you along for years. He knows your weak spots, he knows where you have surrendered ground to him and he's built strongholds there.

The NASB version of 2 Corinthians 10:5 says that 'speculations' and 'lofty things' set themselves up against the knowledge of God. The clear implication is that these are baseless, arrogant lies. These things dominating you are not truth but arguments about truth and pretensions to truth. In the power of God they can be utterly destroyed. Praise God!

For example, if I come into a fearful situation, and that has been my weakness, and I begin to think fearful thoughts, it is because I have yet to take that thought captive and make it submit to the truth in Christ.

So Paul says we take *every* thought captive. There is land to be fought over in your mind – that's the battleground; let us make sure we are taking every thought that runs across that land prisoner. Catch them quickly! Make them submit to the lordship of Christ.

The helmet of salvation

We find the helmet of salvation in Ephesians 6:17. When the Bible talks about salvation, it speaks of it in two contexts. One context is the salvation that is justification by faith; the other context is in the area of an outworking in life. It's a continual salvation – a 'being saved' if you like.

You are continually being saved, but you are not being continually born again, again and again. Righteousness is a gift; it's the grace of God. You are justified and made right with God. It's yours. But the salvation process needs to go on and on in your life.

God wants to save you in your intellect and in your emotions now, as well as giving you a new body in the life to come. He is not 'saving souls', He is saving people. Salvation needs to enter every part of your life.

When Paul talks about the helmet of salvation he is talking about your mind. Salvation needs to come to your thinking. Christians have been born again, but many struggle because salvation has not yet reached into their minds.

There are areas of your mind where Satan can land with impunity – landing strips, if you like, where the enemy zooms in and lands again and again. There was nothing there to guard your thinking or to bomb those landing strips, so in he comes.

We're walking along a road and we see something. Zoom! In comes the enemy and our thought life is in sin again. Or a situation arises and in he comes with another lie – zoom! He's landed, and it feels comfortable again because that's the way we always think. We're a sitting target!

We have to bomb these landing strips with the truth about our ongoing salvation in Christ. There has to be craters everywhere so that he cannot land! Take these landing strips captive for Christ! For years, after becoming a Christian I continued to have certain ways of thinking. There were vulnerable areas of my thought life and the enemy knew what thoughts would affect me and pull me down. Gradually over the years, I have recognised these weak areas and have been able to make a stand against the enemy's tactics. I'm not saying I now have total victory in these areas, but I do recognise the danger signs almost straight away.

Into action!

Many Christians who do Bible study on the subject of the mind are surprised, as they dig into the Scriptures, how many references there are to this subject in the New Testament. It is a major part of apostolic doctrine that we discipline our minds. Unfortunately you would be hard-pressed to find many people who speak on this subject regularly today.

Peter says, 'Prepare your minds for action; be self-controlled' (1 Pet 1:13). What is the thrust of this verse? We're in battle here; this is a battleground. Therefore be very positive – prepare your mind for action. Don't drift, says Peter, don't be casual. Gird up your minds, guard your minds, be sober in spirit and in your thinking be self-controlled. Today there seems to be a great deal of attention given to how we are feeling, or whether we have been hurt by someone, or dealing with issues of the past. Scripture, however, simply does not support this emphasis, but does tell us to think right!

Some Christians you look at have such potential, but somehow they never seem to accomplish what God has for them and they never really go anywhere in Christ. So often it is because they are laid-back sort of people. I'm sure you know the type. They tend to be casual, laid-back, friendly and fun. Actually, they are also casual in their thinking and laid-back about the battle in their minds; casual about whether or not they have their armour on and drifting about the battlefield with exposed heads!

Can you see that that is contrary to the Scriptures? That is the root of their problem: their minds are not prepared for action. The same message appears in 1 Peter 5:8: 'Be self-controlled and alert. Your enemy the devil prowls around like a roaring lion looking for someone to devour.'

This is not a game. Many of us fall in the area of the mind simply because we are lazy and ill-disciplined. We can't be bothered. You will be sniped at by the enemy and picked off if you have a casual approach to the way you think.

Recognise, too, that Satan is a liar and a deceiver. He won't jump out at you with horns and a spear and a big S on his

T-shirt. You'd recognise him then! He's also a deceiver, so he disguises himself as something OK and reasonable. In Ephesians 6 Paul speaks about us fighting, not against flesh and blood, but against principalities and powers. But where do we fight these battles? It seems to me, from this passage, that principalities and powers are so like flesh and blood that we can have the two easily confused. In other words, principalities and powers are very much at work in a 'down to earth' context – not some 'mystical, out of reach, other force'!

If principalities and powers are at work, then my mind is a classic target for them. If I think wrong thoughts about my church, if I harbour unforgiveness in my thinking from events that have happened in the past, if I think wrong thoughts about my leaders and therefore allow undermining attitudes to develop – see how much ground those principalities and powers have gained. If I change the way I think, I pull down, I fight those powers and overcome wrong thoughts. Remember Satan's goal is to deceive you.

For example, when you are tempted to think a wrong lustful thought, he lies to you. He says, 'Come on, imagine! It'll give you a good time, it will satisfy you and you'll feel all the better for it.'

Rubbish! We know it satisfies only for a moment and then comes condemnation. We know it doesn't fulfil us, but cuts us off from God and our walk with Him. Eventually, it devours and destroys us.

A lot of people blame the devil for their terrible days and weeks and persist in thinking they need deliverance. Actually they don't need deliverance, they need resistance.

Resistance to that first thought. Bomb that landing strip, and make some craters around here!

'I'm so glad it's only the devil. We can deal with that straight away.'

'But surely I need hours of ministry and deep, deep inner healing?'

'No, it's only the devil. No problem, he's only a liar and he's just conned you for a moment. Let's speak the truth about this.'

'But I've booked myself out for three hours with you!'

'Well, you might need that to learn some Scripture. Learn the truth, and speak it to your mind.'

Your mind has been recaptured by Christ. He has the authority now.

The devil has only one weapon he can use on you in the battle for the mind. *Temptation*. Whether he is successful in that temptation or not is dependent upon how much room we give to temptation in our thinking. It is no good running to your small group leader or even your elders and pastors, saying: 'Please take my thoughts captive for me because I can't deal with them.' They can't do it for you. You must do it for yourself.

James says, 'Submit yourselves, then, to God. Resist the devil and he will flee from you' (James 4:7).

Simple, isn't it? It's a promise of God, there in the Bible in black and white. The promise isn't that he'll just slink away in a corner and sulk. The promise is: he will flee from you.

He speeds off as fast as he can go. He disappears. He vanishes. His presence is no longer with you.

Remember, he's a liar. Start to see his words as lies and

resist him. He has said to the nation: 'Worship the god of sex. Give yourself to this god and you will be satisfied.' But he doesn't tell the other side of the story. He doesn't tell of children's heartbreak as families split; he doesn't talk of thousands of ruined lives, of VD and AIDS, of abortion and the degradation of prostitution. The end result is misery. He is a liar and the father of lies.

5. Replacement, Not Removal!

How not to succeed: many Christians have a major misconception. They think that temptation is best defeated by concentrating on it. They believe that taking the thought captive for Christ requires intense concentrated effort.

For instance, you might have a lust problem. (If you are worried about anger, envy, fear, etc., just delete 'lust' and put in your word.) Having got thus far with this book, you feel ready to hit this. Your thinking goes something like this: 'Now, I've got to renew my mind, therefore I must get rid of this lustful thought. Lustful thought – I won't think it. Go away, lust! I rebuke you, lust. I rebuke you, lust. I won't think of you, lustful thought. I won't have you, lustful thought. I stand against lust.'

What has happened here? You have a person whose mind is dominated by lust. It's filling every moment. The enemy has trapped him into concentrating on his problem, not on the truth. Whole periods of time are spent in futile battle with only one thing on his mind – lust!

Try this test out on a friend – preferably one who hasn't done this or heard of it before!

Stage 1: Get them to sit still, close their eyes and think. Just think. Anything will do. Do that for a few moments.

Stage 2: Now tell your friend that whatever happens, under no circumstances must he or she think of white mice. It is strictly forbidden to think of white mice. Lay it on thick now; describe the white whiskers, the pink nose twitching, the long tail, but keep insisting to your friend that white mice must not be considered.

Stage 3: Suddenly switch to grey elephants. Don't think about grey elephants. Lay it on as thick as before. Crashing through the undergrowth, huge trunks, big ears, look at those tusks! But under no circumstances think about grey elephants.

Stage 4: What happened to the white mice?

This is the principle for winning the battle. You have a wrong thought. How are you going to deal with that wrong thought? *Fill your mind with right thoughts and the wrong thoughts go.* If I have a lust problem, I deliberately fill my mind with thoughts that are good, pure and right before God. With my mind dominated by truth, and understanding that these lustful thoughts are full of lies anyway and they won't do me any good, I find they simply bounce off me and are gone.

No vacuum

A renewed mind does not just consist of ridding yourself of old thoughts. You need to replace those old thoughts with new ones. If we simply take the old thoughts captive we will be left with a vacuum. The enemy just loves vacuous people. Here is a very fertile ground for his temptations – a blank mind!

If you leave a vacuum the old thoughts will return again and again. This is a major cause of the ups and downs which many Christians suffer. I can rebuke the fearful thought. I can tell it Bible verses and I can see it flee, but if I don't replace it with fresh, godly thinking I leave myself wide open to the return trip. Round it comes again, a fearful thought with its landing lights blazing, looking for a nice bit of vacuous mind for a trouble free touchdown.

The Scriptures

We need to exchange those thoughts taken captive for Christ with right thoughts. The Bible is very clear about that. Paul exhorts us, 'Set your minds on things above, not on earthly things' (Col 3:2). He also lists the sort of things he wants us to think about: whatever is true, noble, right, pure, lovely, admirable, excellent or praiseworthy (Phil 4:8). He also says, 'Let the word of Christ dwell in you richly' (Col 3:16) and 'Continue to live in him, rooted and built up in him' (Col 2:6,7).

Successful substitution comes from being rooted and grounded in Christ's Word, having a new mind set, dwelling on godly things in a positive way. Encourage yourself into biblical thought patterns. If your mind is full of the truth of God there's no room for the enemy to land. He comes in with his lies, landing lights on to attract attention, but he simply has to do a circuit and fly back to where he comes from. That is the result of a mind set on things above, dwelling on the truth.

Ceaseless traffic

We need to recognise that ungodly thoughts have ploughed through our minds in ceaseless traffic for years. Attitudes and habitual reactions have formed a cavalcade of unrighteous thinking. Illustrated like that, we begin to see how deeply ingrained these thoughts have been.

We have all seen those deeply rutted farm tracks, haven't we? Day in, day out, in all weathers, for years and years the farmer has taken his tractor and trailer and his Range Rover up and down the track. Up and down, up and down. The result is two deep ruts worn firmly (or muddily!) into the ground, clearly defining the wheelbase of his vehicles. The ruts are usually marked by tractor tyres and they're usually rough and bumpy, with a high ridge of grass separating them.

Similarly, your mind has been scored by the ceaseless traffic of ungodly thinking. Your mind is used to it. In fact, it even begins to feel right. It begins to feel comfortable as the enemy cruises down the well-worn ruts in his Range Rover marked 'temptation'. It feels natural to be full of fear, it feels comfortable to be indulging self-pity, and someone only has to make a quick remark and we're off down the track again.

When you become a Christian it's as if you are given a new car. Here you are in your brand new Mini of godly thoughts. Very pleased, you drive swiftly into your mind only to find that the way forward is very uncomfortable. Your Mini doesn't fit the ruts! At best you'll bump along at first; you might even get stuck on the grass ridge, wheels spinning!

Is that your experience? Godly thoughts rise uneasily in your mind. They even appear alien to its environment.

The solution is not to throw away the car, but to drive up and down the tracks of your mind incessantly in your godly thoughts vehicle. You now need a cavalcade of godly thoughts – up and down, up and down. You need to do this continuously to create new ruts of thinking in your mind. New tracks that will bias your mind towards righteousness; a new environment in your attitudes, so that it is the ungodly thoughts which become out of place and uncomfortable in the new righteous ruts of your mind. Those old wheels won't fit the new course on which you are set; they're in for a rough ride.

Know the right thoughts

'Fine,' you say. 'I'm with you thus far. That's a great illustration, but I don't know what the right thoughts are. I don't know the truth to apply in these situations.'

For many of us, brought up in very legalistic situations, it was one of the great eye-openers of the charismatic movement that God, in His grace, was not watching over us with a big stick to make sure we read our Bibles every morning between 6.00am and 6.30am.

What liberty! What release! We discovered the heavens didn't fall in if we didn't manage to read anything for a whole week. Then a month, then a year! What liberty! Until, one day, we discover that the issue isn't Bible reading actually, but knowing what the Word of God says. We discover that we need to be soaking ourselves in the Scriptures, taking every opportunity to read what God says in His Word.

If we do not know the Word of truth, how are we going to counteract lies? If we have not got a ready armoury of the truth of God we are not even going to go into battle, let alone win it. If we are not saturating ourselves in truth, how are we going to create mind-changing cavalcades of it?

The Bible isn't a passive book – it's not just words on a page. It's God speaking to me; it's truth that will penetrate my heart and mind. It will change me. It is not a case of having to read the Bible every day. The issue is this: when you realise you can't live without the Word of God, you can't get enough of it. Each day there are battles to be fought and battles which will be won if the truth of God dwells in you.

Agree with God

We need to agree with the things God says about us. You need to know His attitude towards you and how He sees you, rather than how you see yourself.

Stop agreeing with your pessimistic, cynical, passive self

and start agreeing with God and His vibrant, glorious, certain, secure view of who you are in Him. It goes something like this. The enemy whispers to you that God does not love you. 'God sees everything you do so how could He possibly love you? He doesn't even like you! Oh, by the way – none of His people like you either!'

These are all lies – they all contradict the absolute truth. God does love you! Even with your failings and your inconsistencies. It's time to line up with truth. Does God love me? Yes! 'But God, rich in mercy, because of his great love, made us alive with Christ even when we were dead in our sins' (Eph 3:4,5). Our minds should be filled with His ability, His power, His authority, His determination to see us changed. Paul says that we 'are being transformed into his likeness with ever-increasing glory, which comes from the Lord, who is the Spirit' (1 Cor 3:18).

Obviously there is not space here to quote suitable Scripture verses for every fear, phobia or temptation. In any case we need to be familiar, not just with particular verses, but with great themes of our relationship with God which run through the Scriptures. We can look at some examples, though, to give you the flavour of how to approach things.

Fears

Suppose you are afraid of the dark. Many people are, and often it first begins with a traumatic experience in childhood. You can have ministry for that, you can be delivered from the stronghold of Satan which he has built up on the back of that experience, but what you need for continuing in victory is the Word of God. It needs to be saturating your mind. Now comes the moment! You are alone in the house one evening, clearing up. You have to go out to the dustbin – in the dark! But here comes the Word of God, which declares, 'You will not fear the terror of night . . . nor the pestilence that stalks in the darkness' (Ps 91:5,6). 'Surely I am with you always, to the very end of the age' (Matt 28:20). Romans 8:38,39 sums up the phrases with one sentence: 'Nothing will be able to separate us from the love of God that is in Christ Jesus our Lord.'

You must decide: either these were nice thoughts and pleasant poetry written many centuries ago or they are the Word of God that will pierce you and fill you and make you more than a conqueror. They are full of the power of God even today.

Phobias

Maybe you have a phobia about flying. I struggled with this in earlier years as a Christian. I'm off to the USA, for instance, in a great big, beautiful, super-smooth 747. Up to 30,000 feet the fear comes. Then the recall of all those films: *Airport 77, 78, 79*, then they ran out of numbers – planes with dead pilots, planes under the water, and planes without wings. The series became ridiculous in the end. But I remember and fear grips me. I sit sweating, panicky and wretched.

Decision time. Either this happens every time I fly – and remember I've got to get back home the same way – or I renew my mind and fill it with God's Word. John 16:33, for example: 'I have told you these things so that in me you may have peace. In this world you will have trouble. But take heart! I have overcome the world.'

'Wonderful! You have overcome the world, Lord. That means You're in control here. My life isn't in the enemy's hands, it's in God's hands.'

Philippians 1:21 is also very relevant here: 'For to me, to live is Christ and to die is gain.'

'Great, if the plane goes down I'm OK. In fact it'll be even better for me. I'm at peace with my Lord. Hey! This journey is quite pleasant after all. Pass the steak.' In fact, whatever potential phobia you may face, this principle is the same. Once in the potential phobic situation you can there and then remind yourself of God's Word, even mumble it under your breath if necessary. You'll be amazed. It works!

Under pressure

Some years ago I was very ill. The doctors couldn't find anything wrong. Tests followed more tests, but all were inconclusive. I was out of action for about a year with this unknown illness. I felt low, I felt that no one understood me and I felt isolated. Fertile ground for the enemy. My mind could have been wide open, with landing strips the width of three motorways. But I began to fill my mind with the Word of God.

Go further than that: be ready to speak out to others relevant scriptures for their situations. Minister to others what you minister to yourself.

This doesn't have to be intense and super-spiritual. You don't have to be a kind of biblical robot walking around quoting verses at everything and everyone. People like that are simply living in unreality. You don't have to be like those actors who play Jesus in the films, gazing with glazed superholy expressions into camera 3 while speaking in a slow, deep, sonorous voice. When people say: 'I can't,' say, 'Look, the Word of God says you can do all things through Christ who strengthens you' (Phil 4:13).

When they say, 'I'm defeated,' say: 'God always leads us in triumph through Christ' (2 Cor 2:14).

'I'm scared of the devil.' No: 'Greater is he that is in you than he who is in the world' (1 Jn 4:4).

'God doesn't love me.' What! 'There is therefore now no condemnation for those in Christ Jesus' (Rom 8:1).

Confess the Word of God to yourself and to others. This is not the power of positive thinking, or mind over matter. It is simply ensuring that the Word of God becomes part of your thinking, making new tracks in your mind, and giving the enemy a really rough time.

6. The Sword – Expose the Root

When we want to know about our weaponry in spiritual warfare we naturally turn to Ephesians 6. In that passage only one piece of equipment is for offensive use, the rest are defensive. That weapon is 'the sword of the Spirit which is the Word of God' (Eph 6:17).

Now isn't that interesting? Just what we have been looking at in the last chapter. The sword is a weapon of war. It's used to attack the enemy. The Bible is very clear on this point: we attack the enemy with the Word of God. Jesus did it in the wilderness. The Word of God was already filling His mind ready to be brought swiftly and appropriately into play.

The sword cuts straight through, no messing about. It's not for display purposes, to be hung on a wall and gazed at. No, it's for action. It enables us to go on the offensive. The Word of God is our weaponry to pull down strongholds, to cut away the lies of the enemy, to renew our thinking and to guard our minds from further attack.

Hebrews 4:12 says that the Word of God is living and active, sharper than any double-edged sword. Let us look at the two edges of this sword of the Word, which will be effective in renewing the mind. The first, which we will deal with in this chapter, is that the sword gets to the root of the problem, cuts it out and sorts you out. The second, the subject of Chapter 7, is that the sword exposes the enemy and thrusts him through.

Exposing the root

Hebrews 4:12 says, 'The word of God is living and active. Sharper than any double-edged sword, it penetrates even to dividing soul and spirit, joints and marrow; it judges the thoughts and attitudes of the heart.'

That describes a pretty lethal weapon. It pushes right through to the thoughts and the attitudes of the heart. That's radical.

If we're honest, many Christians don't see the Word of God like that at all. They find it boring, irrelevant and often dull, and they don't realise that actually it is awesome, and that it reveals mercilessly the intentions of people's hearts.

Often, then trying to help others, we experience problems because first we don't know the Word of God well enough, secondly we are not practised at using what we do know, and thirdly we are scared of upsetting people. We want to be nice and understanding, cosy and chatty. We don't like upsetting people and we want to be popular.

Having a chat, waffling on, even having a bit of a debate about an issue doesn't get to the root and deal with it. The

Word of God, correctly applied, will expose the root. It can be painful and distressing sometimes and it certainly won't leave you untouched, but it is supremely effective in dealing with your motives.

How many prophecies do you hear? How many can you remember? You remember the ones that spoke the Word of God to you, that cut through to roots, that caused change in your life. Sometimes you can't remember them from a week ago, but you can remember ones that really spoke to you years back. That's the power of the Word of God that flowed in them. Scripture is even more powerful.

Four root problems

Four particular areas of attitude in the heart are common to people who are in difficulties in their minds: passivity, pride, lack of faith and lack of devotion.

Passivity

This is a heart attitude that can dominate the mind, making us lethargic and slow to respond, unable and unwilling to stir ourselves. As a result we constantly fail to hit targets and meet goals in our lives.

Often it is exacerbated by overfamiliarity. If you are over-familiar with the Word of God your attitude will be: I've heard it all before. I know that. As a result, the Word bounces off you. It never penetrates into you because it hits a wall, a wall of passivity, and simply bounces off again. People with this problem of passivity can become apathetic and lazy, unprepared to stir themselves and sharpen their thinking.

Proverbs 24:30–34 tells us that the field of a sluggard is covered with thorns and weeds and that its wall is in ruins. The sluggard comes to poverty and ruin.

No wonder the enemy tries to make it as difficult as possible for us to spend time meditating on God's Word. It is a problem nearly all Christians face at some time or other. We pick up our Bibles and immediately we can think of four or five different things that are suddenly pressing matters that need to be dealt with at once. Sometimes we would even rather attend to the washing up!

Then, when we have settled down to it, we have difficulty concentrating. There's a battle on. We become sleepy and inattentive, we read a passage and nothing goes in. Our eyes have slid over the words and our minds have let the meaning of them slip by like a dream. We have become dulled and overfamiliar. We know that these words can come to life, we know that fresh insight and faith-stirring revelation can come from the most well-worn pages of our Bibles, but through a passive heart attitude the enemy steals away the potential for fruitfulness.

The problem in most people's lives is apathy, despite an 'upwardly mobile' minority. Look at your neighbours for evidence. Many will have stopped living and now just exist in a day-to-day humdrum. Ask yourself the question: how much of that passive, apathetic attitude have I taken on board? It seems to me that for the Christian church in the UK, passivity has become a very real stronghold – a genuine scheme of the enemy to prevent us from becoming the type of people we are meant to be. What is the opposite to passivity? Answer? Passion! Many of us have a heart to be genuinely passionate about God and his purposes and yet we find this 'cloud of passivity' all around us. It begins so often in the way we think. Even the first few thoughts when you first wake up can determine whether or not today will be another passive, careless day or a day of passionate achievement.

God's Word is a mighty weapon of passion. To defeat a stronghold (e.g. passivity) you need to enter into combat. It won't just fade away. You will need to fight, wrestle, struggle, rebuke, resist – these are all biblical phrases describing our need to shrug off passivity. I have watched Christians on many occasions take a step forward to restore passion for God. Three weeks later they are back to where they started. Why? In their desire to respond to passion, they soon hit the cloud of passivity and rather than battling on through, learning to simply overcome, they gave up. In the Western world this is a major stronghold in our minds.

Christian living is supposed to be a life full of adventure. How, then, can we be passive and successful in our lives? So often we see Christians with all the potential and all the gifting, but they are passive and lazy. They don't have a sense of personal responsibility and accountability for what they hear. The result is that the Word of God does not penetrate their life and their thinking.

Jesus said, 'From everyone who has been given much, much will be demanded; and from the one who has been entrusted with much, much more will be asked' (Lk 2:48). We are so fortunate to have access to so much teaching, to so many books and tapes and so on. We say that we're pioneers, we're moving on in God, but the word to the passive is: just how true is that of you? Don't let's kid ourselves.

When you come before Him and He says: 'What about your family? It was such a mess,' you will not be able to reply that no one was available to advise you at the time. Most telling of all, you will not be able to say that you didn't have the Word of God. You can see films and videos, read books and listen to tapes; you can go to seminars and hear it on Sunday, but the issue is: has the Word of God penetrated your life?

Remember our verse, Luke 12:48? The converse must also be true. Five people sitting faithfully in the pews of a chapel somewhere and only hearing liberal theology every Sunday will not have much required of them. We are responsible for what we hear and there is no room for passivity.

Jesus repeated a certain phrase often: 'He who has ears, let him hear' (Matt 13:9). Every time you hear the Word proclaimed or study the Scriptures, ask the Lord to cause it to penetrate. Say to yourself, 'I want this to penetrate. I'm responsible for what I'm hearing and reading and I want to do something about it.' We can have churches full of hearers who are only half-listening, but it is those who 'hear' with every fibre of their being, and who are 'doers' of the Word, who are the ones actually receiving it. The parable of the man who built his house upon the rock as opposed to the one who built his house on sand is not a comparison of the foundations laid in a believer as opposed to an unbeliever. But rather it was spoken to all who were listening and at least potentially followers of Jesus. Those who hear and do nothing are building lives on sands. Those who hear and apply that which they have heard are building secure lives, as a rock.

To update this – you hear a powerful word on Sunday morning on 'being secure in the sovereignty of God'. You hear it clearly – but this is of little advantage if the content of that word is not applied to your life during the rest of that week. When potential 'insecurity' comes along we then discover whether or not you are merely a hearer of the Word or a doer! This is allowing God's Word to penetrate your thinking. This is the opposite to remaining passive.

Deliberately shrug off passivity and laziness. When the word on Sunday is about a familiar subject, refuse that thinking which says, 'I've heard it all before. I know this already.' Actively seek more from it, have an attitude and a posture which speaks of your desire to receive fresh impetus in your life even in the familiar areas.

The parable of the sower focuses on *receptivity*. It's the state of the soil which counts. The seed is the same wherever it lands. Good soil is the lives of people who are able to receive again and again. The density of the crop is dependent on the receptivity of the soil.

Pride

Pride is another heart attitude which will really mess up your mind. Peter says, 'Clothe yourselves with humility towards one another' (1 Pet 5:5). We need this attitude in us because we will be hearing the Word of God again and again. In order to receive it and see it begin to change me and renew my mind, I am going to need humility.

Teaching people who are proud is impossible. There are three main reasons:

1. Proud people come with preconceived ideas. It means that they have formed an opinion or an idea of what they believe beforehand. Speaking to them is pointless because their minds are made up.
2. Proud people are presumptuous. They presume that their understanding is correct. They already know the truth of the matter. They can handle this, there is nothing you can teach them they don't already know, and, what's more, they have more experience than you anyway!
3. Proud people don't listen. Either they switch off in a self-righteous cloud of smugness, barely aware of what is being said; or they sit on the edge of their seat waiting to pounce on the first 'mistake', prejudging the course of the word and often 'hearing' things that haven't been said.

Do you know people like that? That's easy, we all seem to know someone like that. The more important question is: do you recognise yourself here?

Be clothed with humility, be receptive, be good soil whether listening to preaching or reading the Word.

In Proverbs there is an often repeated phrase which is translated in the Authorised Version: 'incline thine ear'. In the New International Version the translation of that phrase is most often 'pay attention'. The couplet to it usually says something like 'apply your heart'. To see examples of this look at Proverbs 2:2; 4:20; 5:1; 22:17.

Here is an exercise for you: try to incline your ear without moving your head! Some of us can twitch our ears up and down, but to incline our ears actually requires us to bow our heads. We have to make a movement which, in effect, is an attitude of submission and an acknowledgement of the superior.

So these verses are saying something very profound; they're saying that we need to have a heart attitude of humility to be able to hear properly.

We have two options when we read the Word. We can either let the familiar words slip easily across the mind – the pleasing poetry, the easy phrase with the nice ring to it – or we can sit down and get stuck in, taking it phrase by phrase and applying it to ourselves.

Approaching the Bible humbly is an important exercise when you live in a proud, presumptuous, so-called 'reasonable' age. Culture and modern intellectualism convince us they are right. If Christians are moulded by this attitude they will surely have great problems in receiving God's Word in humility.

Lack of faith

The message the Israelites heard was of no value to them because they did not combine it with faith (Heb 4:2). We can listen to the Word, we can be intent on it, but it will remain just words to us if our heart attitude is not one of faith. Without faith in the Word, it will not be fruitful in us. We must mix what we hear with faith, otherwise it remains ineffective.

For example, we can hear about signs and wonders at a conference, but it will be just notes in a notebook, words on a tape and jargon in a book unless our heart attitude is to believe it. We must be ready to receive it as truth, to let it penetrate our thinking, to let it be tied in and twinned with faith.

Otherwise all that will remain will be dry verses unrelated to life, and the opportunities will have been lost.

Lack of devotion

Here is a fourth heart attitude which can be a root problem. A lack of devotion forms a barrier to the presentation of the Word of God.

Acts 2:42 says, 'They devoted themselves to the apostles' teaching and to the fellowship, to the breaking of bread and to prayer.'

When the Word of God comes to you, it may break through passivity and pride, and it may break through your lack of faith, because you are beginning to build that into your life, but there is often this final barrier of a lack of devotion. One verse speaks of the devotion of those first Christians. That they devoted themselves 'continually' is the emphasis of the New American Standard Bible translation.

We need to give ourselves utterly to whatever God is highlighting to us. For example, if it is a lack of faith then I will give myself to the pursuit of faith. I will read books, listen to tapes, and I will put myself alongside people of faith and drain them dry of everything they know, following their example. I am on a mission to get faith into my life.

With this attitude we will not be content to float and drift through life. It will not be enough to say: 'Yes, I'm thinking about faith. I'm meditating on it a little.' No, we must devote ourselves to the Word of God.

Paul exhorts us not to be like others who are asleep, but like those who are alert and self-controlled (1 Thess 5:6). He asks Timothy to be diligent, to give himself to such things so that everyone would see his progress (1 Tim 4:15).

Look at it this way: life is too short to let it drift by and to waste it on passivity, pride, lack of faith and lack of devotion. The Word of God is a sword. It is a weapon of attack. First, let it attack you. Let it cut into you and expose those areas of your life that need to be transformed.

7. The Sword – Expose the Enemy

Remember, we are now pitched into the centre of the battle for the mind. We have seen how God's Word is a sword which can pierce through and deal with our own heart attitudes. If they are not dealt with they will trip us up and cause us to suffer defeats in the battle.

The sword is also an offensive weapon for attacking the enemy. It can be wielded by us to refute the lies of Satan. Remember that we saw the issue was not just avoiding wrong thoughts, but replacing those wrong thoughts with the Word of God and what He says about us.

If we are saturated in the Word of God, if it has been penetrating our thinking and our mind has been trained to be set on the things of the Spirit, then Satan has a problem! As he comes in to do battle and try to reclaim the ground he has lost, ground that was once under his control, he finds instead the Word of God like a sword flashing out at him. In every direction he turns he will see row upon row of swords ready to run him through!

The sword of the Word of God is in your mind. It is an offensive weapon set to attack and ready to penetrate the lies of the enemy and expose him for what he is. The enemy has been dethroned, and now we have the mind of Christ. He has no hold over us; we have died to ourselves and our lives are hidden with Christ in God. That is wonderful, but the enemy will come back at us again and again with his one weapon. Let us spend some time learning about this one and only weapon: temptation.

From over the horizon

The enemy doesn't own any camps in your mind. He has been ousted by Jesus. You have been placed by God 'in him'. In Ephesians 1:4–14 the words 'in him' appear four times, reminding us that we have been transferred from one kingdom to another. We have been chosen in Him before the creation of the world to be holy and blameless in His sight (1:4). We have redemption and forgiveness in Him in accordance with the riches of His grace (1:7). We are chosen in Him and predestined by His will in order that we might be for the praise of His glory (1:11,12). We have been included in Christ and sealed in Him by the Holy Spirit (1:13).

We haven't been left to drift; we have been placed in Him. We are protected by Him and empowered by the Holy Spirit. The devil doesn't have any rights or authority over you or your thinking. He doesn't reign any more; he's out there with his solitary weapon, hoping to fly in over the horizon, under your radar, and catch you off guard with his lies.

Sortie objectives

As he flies in, he has one weapon and one objective: to take back ground he has lost. He wants to use temptation to re-establish a bridgehead in your mind. He wants to get back his grip on some corner of your mind.

The landing place

Temptation is the weapon Satan uses as he hovers over your thinking. Temptation begins with a thought in your mind. It is Satan's point of entry, and if he is having a heyday in our thinking it is because we haven't yet learned how to deal with tempting thoughts. There are areas of our mind where the sword of the Word is not pointing menacingly at the enemy, ready to repulse any salvo of temptation.

The end result

The end result that Satan is looking for is that you might be enticed into sin. He may start by speaking just a little thought and lying to you that if you dwell on it, it will be satisfying, relieve the pressure, give you a thrill inside – or whatever – but his end result will be sin in your life.

James says, 'Each one is tempted when, by his own evil desire, he is dragged away and enticed. Then, after desire has conceived, it gives birth to sin; and sin, when it is full-grown, gives birth to death' (Jas 1:14,15).

In these verses we see that James, like Paul in Romans 6:11,12, has a radical but biblical view of Christian living which is not very common: you don't have to sin! In fact the normal Christian life is to walk with God; sin should be a rare interruption, not a regular occurrence.

John says, 'If we confess our sins he is faithful and just and will forgive our sins and purify us from all unrighteousness' (1 Jn 1:9).

The Word is clear: you will always be able to go to the throne of grace and receive total, utter forgiveness. The problem is that many people live defeated lives. They seem to be on a continuous cycle: sin, confession, forgiveness, sin; round and round. We have a forgiving God and He will forgive and forgive. The sacrifice Jesus made will always be sufficient to atone for every sin. But the devil has got a foothold, a landing strip, a corner of your mind with ready access for him to be successful with his one weapon of temptation.

God wants us to live and walk with Him continually. The enemy knows that and his objective is to keep interrupting that as often and as regularly as he can. He does that by enticing us to sin as often as he can. In that way he can keep us immature, he can keep us condemned and ineffective and he can draw us away from the fullness of what God wants for us.

The characteristics of temptation

Having seen how the enemy deploys his weaponry, let us spend a little time having a closer look at the weapon itself. This is very important because it will help you to be more accurate with your sword!

Temptation is nice

There is no point in the devil tempting us with thoughts and ideas that we find obnoxious or revolting. We wouldn't fall for it, would we? It is amazing how many people overlook this simple fact and its implications. What is presented to you must have some attraction to you at some level or other. Often it is seemingly true and it has the appearance of being acceptable. Often it accentuates the pleasure and fails to remind you of the penalties and the misery that will follow. Satan is a liar and a schemer. The Bible acknowledges this.

Hebrews 11:25 tells us that Moses joined the Israelites rather than enjoy the pleasures of sin for a short time (Heb 11:25).

If everyone were to receive 100 volts of electricity every time they were tempted we wouldn't enjoy the process much. Not many of us would run to embrace the prospect. Satan knows that, so temptation comes with a smile and an enticement. To try to identify it by whether it feels all right will be a very unreliable indicator. Rather we need to recognise it by comparison with the Word of God.

Luke 4:1–4 gives us an example of temptation in action. Jesus was hungry and Satan was giving Him the opportunity to eat. It was a very attractive proposition, but only in the short term.

Temptation is not sin

Here is another radical but true fact about the devil's weapon which we must understand for successful warfare.

To suffer temptation, to have that first thought invade your mind, is not the same thing as committing sin.

Some Christians find themselves in all sorts of turmoil because they are tempted. Yet if we look at Hebrews we find very clear statements about the life Jesus led and how He too was tempted. We remember that Jesus was tempted in the wilderness after His baptism in a special way, but we often forget that He was tempted in *every* area of life. It is crucial for us to understand this.

Hebrews 4:15 tells us that Jesus was 'tempted in every way, just as we are – yet was without sin'. He knows about your temptations. He lived through life bombarded by the enemy's lies and guilt, yet He lived through it without giving in once to those temptations. He accomplished what Adam failed to do – live a life without sin – so that He became that second victorious Adam in the fight.

Hebrews 2:18 tells us that Jesus was tempted – and suffered because of it. Temptations didn't always bounce off Jesus without Him noticing. They were not like water off a duck's back to Him. He too had to 'suffer' the process of recognising, determining and dealing with temptation. He too had to suffer the antagonism of the enemy as he tried to break down godliness and righteousness wherever he saw it.

We need to recognise that at the point when we have a thought, nothing has happened. For instance, suppose I am on a diet. I am walking through the shops and the thought of eating a chocolate eclair comes into my mind. The picture in my mind is clear: cream oozing out, thick, dark chocolate on top – I can almost taste it!

That is temptation. But if I dwell on that idea, if I run the thought round and round in my mind, if I begin to salivate, I'm in trouble. I will begin to decry my diet and make excuses to myself as to why it would be OK to enjoy just one eclair.

In no time at all, I find my steps taking me, as if by magic, to the cake shop. Somehow I'm inside, and somehow, strangely, as if it's someone else, I find myself asking for eclairs. Lo and behold! In two minutes all that is left to remind me of eclairs is:

Exhibit A: an empty paper bag smudged with chocolate.

Exhibit B: a sticky mouth surreptitiously wiped by the back of my hand.

Exhibit C: a guilty conscience.

That is succumbing to temptation, letting it dominate my thinking and turn me to sin. Inevitably the sin bore fruit in sinful action. But remember, the first thought was not sin, it was temptation. And, what is more, *temptation that could have been dealt with.*

Temptation never goes away

Another point we need to understand about temptation is that it never goes away. If you think that one day you will be living the perfect life and Satan will sink away into the background, you are very mistaken. There is no such thing as a temptationless state this side of death.

Some people think that Jesus, after being tempted by Satan in the wilderness, then went through the rest of His life in a sort of holy haze. Yet as we study the Bible we see that He continually faced temptations. The enemy came back again and again.

In fact, as we look at the Garden of Gethsemane, we find there that Jesus went through a very real and substantial battle with temptation. There was a battle on in the mind. As His ministry reached its climax, as the cross and its agonies loomed ahead, so Jesus fought against the temptation to turn back from God's purposes.

Luke's account in Luke 22:39–46 is very graphic. Many temptations lay ahead for the disciples here.

We are not going to be rid of temptation. Its intensity will vary perhaps. Sometimes it will be very strong, particularly if we are foolish and place ourselves in its path. Sometimes we may not be too troubled by it, especially if we have shown consistent strength in an area. What is sure, though, is that we must be always alert and ready, for Satan will never give up trying to destroy the life God has brought to us.

Here are some examples of this alertness and the means Satan uses to tempt you to stumble in your Christian walk.

- 2 Corinthians 2:10,11: Lack of forgiveness – Satan tries to outwit us.
- Galatians 6:1: Being tempted while we're trying to help someone else.
- 1 Timothy 3:7: Malicious talking.
- 2 Peter 3:17: Being enticed away from God by others.

There is never room for complacency in this area of temptation. Some young people think that it will all ease off when they are older. A picture is painted of an increasingly relaxed life as we get older. This is unwittingly reinforced by the way we often hear older people talk about the pressures on the younger generation. They look with horror, wondering how Christian young people survive, readily commenting that it was a lot easier in their day.

This is nonsense. We do not slide into cruise control as we pass into middle age. Temptation continues. The form it takes may vary, may be more subtle and less blatant in some areas, but it continues.

Paul says, 'If you think you are standing firm, be careful that you don't fall!'(1 Cor 10:12).

Temptation will be with us for life. Isn't that good news! Temptation is here to stay, so the issue is: what are you going to do about it?

How to counterattack

We've seen how temptation operates, and we've noted two important facts – that temptation in itself is not sin, and that temptation will always be with us as the enemy's only weapon.

Now it's time to go on the counterattack, to move into the offensive. The best form of defence is attack! We have accumulated knowledge about the ways in which the enemy attacks and the capabilities of his weapon. Now we can begin to build our counter-offensive.

The second thought

Here is a key verse which will direct us to the initial manoeuvre of the counterattack. The first part of it goes: 'No temptation has seized you except what is common to man' (1 Cor 10:13).

Sometimes we feel we are in a particularly hopeless position. We feel that no one could possibly have been tempted in quite the same way as we are or with such intensity as we experience. Often people will say things like, 'But you don't know me,' or 'I'm sure no one else is really tempted like me.'

It really is a combination of self-pity and arrogance. Who do you think you are anyway? Unique in the whole human race?! No, of course not. Actually many people are being similarly tempted throughout the world every day.

First Corinthians 10:13 continues, 'And God is faithful; he will not let you be tempted beyond what you can bear.'

The grace of God to us is marvellous, isn't it? There is no temptation beyond our bearing. That's good news, but it leaves us without excuse!

We cannot say, 'It's hopeless, I just can't cope.' We cannot duck out with a lame, 'It just overwhelms me.' This is the truth of God's Word to you and me today – you can resist!

The third sentence of the verse gives us our opportunity for counterattack: 'But when you are tempted, he will also provide a way out so that you can stand up under it.'

With every temptation there's a way of escape. A way out so that you can stand. That's the promise of God to us. There will always be such a way. It doesn't say 'sometimes' or even 'frequently', but it says God will *always* provide a way of escape.

How do we recognise it? If we're to side-step that attack from Satan and start our counter-offensive we must be alert to the opportunity.

My experience is this. Hard on the heels of that first thought – the temptation – comes a second. Almost inseparable, running alongside it, if you like, comes the second thought.

Our once-defiled conscience has come alive again and sends that second thought which says, 'No! Don't!'

If your mind is being renewed and filled with truth, if it's being constantly fed with the Word of God, then immediately the temptation comes the Word of God is there alongside declaring truth back to you.

'It's not right, it's a con, it's a lie. Deal with it straight away like this.'

For instance, you are involved in a conversation and it begins to turn in a way you know isn't right. Immediately after the first thought of temptation calls you to add to the gossip or whatever, in comes the second thought – 'No! Walk away. Take your opportunity and get out now.'

It can be as clear as that. Get out of the situation, move away, cross the street – all ways of escape, practical openings to ensure that temptation doesn't develop into sin. The way of escape is always so practical. The second thought urges us to action. It offers us that first step in successful counterattack.

Second Timothy 2:22 is very simple and direct: 'Flee the evil desires of youth, and pursue righteousness, faith, love and peace, along with those who call on the Lord out of a pure heart.'

Note carefully what it *doesn't* say. It doesn't say, 'Quote Bible verses' at youthful lusts; it doesn't say, 'Debate the validity' of youthful lusts – it just says, 'Run, get out, get away, pronto!'

Take another example. You are watching a favourite programme on television. It finishes and you just sit there a moment – just to see what's next. The programme starts and there are things there you know as a Christian are not for you. What are you going to do about it?

Do you quote Bible verses at the television? Perhaps you should get someone to hold an open copy of the latest Christian magazine in front of the screen? Hope it will go away? Prepare your confession speech now?

No, none of those things will be your second thought. Your third and fourth perhaps, but not your second! Let me tell you your second thought. It's complex theologically, it's very difficult to understand and implement, so note this very carefully.

First you speak to yourself. Say to yourself, 'Rise up from this chair.' Tell your left leg to put one foot forward and then command, with all the power and authority given you, your right leg to do the same. Keep repeating this until you arrive in front of the television set. Now the really difficult bit. Ask your hand, right hand if you're right-handed, to move in the direction of the switch labelled 'on/off'. Move it in the direction of 'off'. And there you are. The television is no longer on and you are no longer tempted!

Of course most of us have found a new miracle gadget – the armchair wizard. It's been especially developed for Christians who suffer temptation from TV programmes. You don't have to do all that I've just described with this gadget – you just sit where you are and with one press of a button – blank screen! Marvellous. A remote way of escape. A way to flee at the greatest pace without even getting up!

Biblical example

It's very interesting to compare David and Joseph when it comes to sexual temptation.

David stood on his roof looking down to where girls bathed. If you do that the high probability is that you will see something. Eyes are powerful instruments. What you see affects your body, your personality, your thinking. David saw. This was the moment of second thought, the moment when conscience says, 'Flee.' But he considered. Then he enquired, then he sent for her, then he entertained her and soon it was lying and murder and scars for the rest of his life (2 Sam 11).

Joseph had a problem. She was Potiphar's wife and she was out to entice him, day after day. One day she manipulated the situation so that she was alone with him. I bet she was at her most alluring as she propositioned him yet again. Did he say, 'Hmm. This is worth considering. Perhaps a coffee and chat might help me decide'? No. The Bible tells us that he fled from her presence – he ran out of the house. He acted on his second thought and made his escape (Gen 39).

Break the habit

We often prefer to ignore the way of escape from temptation and succumb to it instead. Very rarely are our sins isolated incidents. More often they are habitual. We need to break the habit, the vicious circle of temptation and sin, by repeatedly hitting the point of entry. So you must work back from your sin to the original thought, the trigger that propelled you into sin. That is where you will find the way of escape. It's the counterattack move that defeats the enemy.

This process has led many to believe that whatever your past (and therefore your present) habitual state, you can be totally set free. Take a Christian who has been dogged for years by pornography, for instance. What triggered the sinful thoughts? A particular memory? A picture? A person? That individual needs to get hold of those old thoughts and replace them with new ones. Paul says, 'Whatever is true ... noble ... right ... pure ... lovely ... admirable – if anything is excellent or praiseworthy – think about such things' (Phil 4:8). It all happens there in the thought life. You replace the bad images in your mind by thinking about good ones. This applies to any habitual sin: homosexuality, impurity, lust, evil desires and greed. Every time you are tempted to think in a sinful way, deal with the matter at the point of entry and go on doing that whenever you're similarly tempted until your thought process has been transformed.

Let the Word of God dwell in you richly so that you are soaked in it. It's your sword of counterattack, the arouser of conscience, the unmasker of lies. Every time Satan lies to you about all those fears and tensions, about the pleasures of sin for a season, you expose him with the truth of the Word and counterattack – fast!

8. Improving Your Thinking

Charismatic cabbage or creative Christian? We've made our counterattack by using the sword of the Word of God, and we've responded to that nudge from our revitalised conscience. But, as we saw earlier, that isn't enough to start winning the battle. We need now to build the basis of victory from our success in the skirmish. We cannot simply stand in no man's land with our sword limp at our side, our minds in neutral, and expect to survive the enemy's next sortie!

God's aim for everyone is wholeness, not emptiness. Unfortunately, some of us as Christians have problems simply because our minds are empty. We have a very precarious foothold on success if our minds are a vacuum. Remember our verse? 'As a man thinks, so he is' (Prov 23:7). Vacuous mind, vacuous man!

Television is the enormous entertainment success it is because so many people are actually happy to be mindless. We are a society increasingly dominated by visual stimuli as people are content to crash out after work and absorb hours of television. Statistics on the number of hours children watch are frightening. It has enormous power for shaping people's thinking. As we have said before, even the general moral climate portrayed in the many soaps and comedies begins to change our view of what is and what is not acceptable.

It's not just soaps, either. For example, if David Attenborough on television says confidently that this is how things evolved millions of years ago and shows us some fascinating and beautiful wildlife, that's it for the vast majority. No further argument, end of debate – they've seen it on the telly, it must be true.

It's the same, essentially, for many people who work to a background of the radio. Switch it on, switch off the mind. Even DJs have philosophies of life that will inevitably flavour their chatter! Many of us are just mindless absorbers. We let others do our thinking for us. We don't bother to question their values or their arguments.

Many teachers will tell you how endemic this is in our children. They note that more and more students seem unable to ask the question 'Why?' year by year. Their minds have been in neutral. The push-button society has given them incredible ability to manipulate data in computer systems, for instance, but they still have to be trained afresh in the ability to think.

For those involved, say, in the media, the challenges on offer and the environment they are in are full of excitement and continuously stretching. But for us who sit at home and absorb with empty minds, with a vacuum waiting to be filled, it can be devastating to our progress in renewing the mind if we are insufficiently discerning.

This is not an issue of IQ levels or general intellect. This is simply about Christians taking hold of the life God has for them. Because we are born again, because we are right with God, because we have a purpose and a destiny, we should be those who do not dissipate their lives in trivial pursuits and mindless inactivity. Ask yourself the question, 'How creative am I?'

You can meet teenagers whose lives are computer games and television. After five minutes of conversation with you they're finished. It's not because they are naturally dull conversationalists, but they have become dull in their minds. Whatever our age, we can look at and evaluate our leisure time in the same way.

Be honest: how different are you?

A hallmark of the church these days should be creativity. We should be rich together, in our hospitality, in our serving one another, in creativity. We should be those whose accomplishment more than matches our ability. Banish the word 'potential'! Fulfil your potential in Christ!

One way forward for many of us is to read more. Uninformed Christians are so boring! Some used to read more widely and were more informed before they were born again; now they have become dull, and have 'drifted down' to the general level. You were created with the ability to think, dream and imagine and to be expressive with that creativity. Get to it!

Fulfil your potential

So let us purpose to make progress. How can we turn our whole thought process for good? How can we build on our counterattack and begin to fill our minds with the positive thoughts of a vibrant Christian life?

Remember Proverbs 23:7 again. If your mind is filled with godly things you are going to start making those new godly tracks and you're going to be more like Jesus.

So many Christians, as we have seen, are dominated by a negative, pessimistic lifestyle. They never take on new challenges or make any particularly identifiable progress. God didn't create us like animals, just moving by instinct. We have the ability to create, to imagine and to achieve. Our renewed minds can open the way forward for us to fulfil our potential.

There are Christians who have paths ahead of them mapped out by God where they will be mightily effective for Him in society, but they are trapped by unrenewed minds in a vacuum of ever-present 'potential'. Churches are often described as having 'great potential'. We need to be those on a crusade to turn potential into reality.

Paul says, 'Now to him who is able to do immeasurably more than all we ask or imagine, according to his power that is at work in us . . .' (Eph 3:20). The reality of this verse is mind-blowing! Even as we think about things, as our minds are involved in godly issues, so He is able to do all that we are thinking and more. As we ask things of Him, He is able to do all that we ask and more. More exciting still is that He doesn't do these things 'out there', but Scripture is clear that the power is *within* us. He operates within you and me to achieve these things.

This is not the power of positive thinking. It's not will-power. It is the power of God which is fully able, and fully able to do beyond our thoughts and requests. Yes, we are limited in our thinking and wisdom, and God's ways are so much higher than ours, but there is this incredible mystery that God gets right behind our godly thoughts and requests with His almighty power.

The object of renewing your mind is to unclutter your thinking, to clear the ground of the enemy's attacks, so that you can hear the thoughts of God in your mind. We fulfil our potential as we begin to hear and respond to the voice of God in our minds.

When we are transformed from the world and renewed in our thinking we will be able to 'test and approve what God's will is – his good, pleasing and perfect will' (Rom 12:2).

Jesus says, 'My sheep listen to my voice' (Jn 10:27). That voice is not some quiet whisper we strain to hear on the wind from distant fields. It's actually quite clear and strong, but we have been cluttered up with enemy voices and the sound of battle so we have not found it easy to pick out God's voice. Get rid of the clutter and God's voice is clearer. Then the way is open for us to do and to achieve in our Christian lives above the levels we can even imagine at the moment.

Of course, you will make mistakes; know that now, get used to the idea and be ready to pick yourself up and press on. The disciples made plenty of mistakes. Jesus didn't sack them all and replace them with a new group of twelve who were more holy and more perceptive. He just corrected, encouraged and sent them off again.

Next time you are praying in a small group situation, ask

God to give you His thoughts about someone in your group. Don't just pray a nice evangelical prayer. Speak out what God has said in your mind.

This is not a toy to play with – this is the power of God in your life for the extension of His kingdom. We need to act on the thoughts to fulfil our potential.

I remember a lunchtime evangelistic meeting where I fell into conversation with a man who was obviously very bitter and angry and denying the existence of God. We were soon into an amazing debate about who was before God if He did exist, and whether I exist or you are a figment of my imagination, or both. How orange is this chair? What do we mean by 'orange'? If Adam stubbed his toe would it have hurt, etc? The whole works! But all the time a voice in my mind, a thought in my brain, was insistent. Louder and louder it came, that this man had been put out of fellowship in a church because of something he had done.

When he left, I turned to the man next to me who knew him and said, 'That was hard work, wasn't it?' His reply left me stunned. 'Well, you know why? He was asked to leave his church five years ago because he wouldn't repent of his adultery. He went off in a storm of bitterness.' What might have happened had I acted on the thought and fulfilled my potential in that situation!

Watch out! God at work!

Let us back this up with Philippians 2:13: 'For it is God who works in you to will and to act according to his good purpose.'

God is at work in your mind. He is transforming your thinking. Co-operate with Him, work with Him because it is He who is causing you, as you respond, to fulfil His good purposes in you.

Wisdom, knowledge and discernment are all vital today if as Christians we are going to be effective in impacting our generation. All three are promised in Scripture and all three operate in our thinking. A renewed mind thinks wise thoughts and knowledge helps you to apply them. The clearer your thinking, the more discerning you will become in the many complex situations that you find yourself. These attributes are not for the spiritually elite, but for all who will allow their potential to be harnessed by God.

Many of us think God's thoughts without even being fully aware of it. Find out, reach out, step out! You will be amazed. No one can do it for you and you can't do it for others. You can't read it in a book or watch it on a video. In the end you simply have to step out yourself on what you believe God is saying to you.

What a tragedy it is that in most of our churches it is only a nucleus of people, a very small proportion of the membership who actually allow themselves to be stretched in this way. Will you join them?

There will be opportunities in small groups, in meetings, in your street and over your garden fence. God may speak to you about people or about projects. He will teach you about circumstances and events and call you on to new things. Step out! God is at work in you and the more your mind is renewed the more confident you will become.

A person who is thinking like this is hardly mindless or

vacuous – he or she is beginning to discover how improved thinking is fulfilling their potential in Christ. You will be stretched and your gifting will be both more apparent and more fruitful. Watch out! God is at work!

9. Mind Your Mind

We have looked at temptation, we have worked out the strategy to defeat the enemy using the sword of the Word of God and we have begun to build our transformed and renewed mind, filling it with godly thoughts.

Now we need to maintain progress and keep our minds orientated in the right direction. We need a minder for our mind!

The key verse is Romans 8:5: 'Those who live according to the sinful nature have their minds set on what that nature desires.' We have discovered that we can be led by God's Spirit and we have begun to see that we can have the thinking that is characterised as the mind of Christ. The key to keeping things that way is a deliberate act of the will.

In the verse we have just looked at it is called 'setting'. We need to set our minds on the things of the Spirit. It is a determination to lock onto those things. It is as if we have brought them into focus in our aim; now we have to take a decision to lock onto the objective of the things of the Spirit, so that we are immovable. We cannot be bounced off or diverted – we have 'set' our minds (see also Colossians 3:2; Philippians 4:8).

It is as if every day we are challenged – our aim and setting is given a challenge to throw it off course every morning when we wake up. Either we say, 'Father, thank You for this new day. I'm going to live for You and not for myself.' Or else we say, 'Oh!' Yawn. 'I can't be bothered.'

Setting your mind is a daily check of your aim. The decision is yours – check your setting or opt out with lethargy. 'Let your mind dwell on these things,' says Paul. It is a deliberate, conscious act of your will. It is the minder of your mind.

Now we need to make that very practical. What are the ways in which we hold our aim, keep our minds set firmly on the things of the Spirit? I believe there are three things in our daily lives which will help us – to know the Word of God, to be a worshipper and to be supported by other Christians.

1. Set your mind on the Word

Here we are again, back on this crucial subject; knowing what God's Word says about us. We met it before when discussing how to rebut temptation. Here it is once more. The Spirit revels in the promises of God – and so should we. If we are to set our minds on the things of the Spirit there is no doubt that that means delighting ourselves in what God has said.

Please note here what it's *not* about. It's not about floating around in a super-spiritual haze quoting Bible verses incessantly at anything and anyone. When I'm playing football I don't drift around the pitch in a holy glow of meditation. When I'm playing football I'm fully involved mentally, emotionally and physically in running, passing, tackling and (hopefully) scoring goals. Yes, because I'm a Christian I want to play fair and play with a good attitude, but I'm going to play my guts out and be fully involved with my team.

What we're after is a mind-set that, in a sense, runs on autopilot and leaves us free to enjoy life to the full. It's not an invasion of the superspiritual and all the unreality that goes with that sort of approach. Rather it's that we let God infuse our life with His thoughts and priorities so that we are just walking naturally with Him.

The Word of God is effective in many ways. Let us look at some.

It shows you who God is

So many Christians have a problem because they are worshipping someone who is, to all intents and purposes, a stranger to them. They have all sorts of problems with fatherhood, perhaps from their own childhood or from unbalanced teaching in the past.

I have met Christians who believe God is still punishing them for wrong decisions made in the past. Now the God I know isn't like that, but it's often a real battle of persuasion. They need to soak up the truth of what the Bible says about the father heart of God.

It shows you who you are

Each day it's so good to remind ourselves of who we are in Christ. We need to know what our inheritance is, we need to know what our rights are, and we need to know our glorious position in Him. We are liberated from hurt and rejection by realising how God has unashamedly adopted us.

People have all sorts of problems in these areas of acceptance – limited and wrong views of the fullness of our salvation – but they can walk out of these problems simply by believing the Word of God.

It develops effective discipleship

Take a fresh look at yourself. Take a fresh look at the members of your church. As the Holy Spirit draws more and more people into the kingdom of God it will be your responsibility to disciple them. You are called to 'make disciples'. That is an exciting prospect for us all.

However, if you don't know the Word of God, and if your mind is not set on what He says, then what on earth are you going to pass on to others? If you haven't grasped a right picture of God as your Father in heaven, and if you are unsure about your position in Christ, you will have to stand back on the sidelines and watch others do the job of discipling new Christians.

What you are, others will become. That applies negatively as well as positively. If you do not grasp the liberating principles of the grace of God, the chances are that you will bring people unwittingly into legalism. That's because you won't be sharp enough to recognise the symptoms of a legalistic attitude in yourself or others.

Immerse yourself in the Word of God; let it fill your mind and affect your outlook and your behaviour. Then others will not need to make your mistakes – they'll make their own anyway – and they will learn from your example. That is practical discipleship.

It develops your contributions to the body of Christ

Let us look at two different verses where Paul is exhorting people to take their full part in the life of the church.

In two passages of Scripture Paul tells us what his objective is for us:

'Do not get drunk on wine, which leads to debauchery. Instead, be filled with the Spirit. Speak to one another with psalms, hymns and spiritual songs. Sing and make music in your heart to the Lord' (Eph 5:18,19).

'Let the word of Christ dwell in you richly as you teach and admonish one another with all wisdom, and as you sing psalms, hymns and spiritual songs with gratitude in your hearts to God' (Col 3:16).

The sources of this activity are the Spirit and the Word. They yield the same fruit and the same result. We need both of these routes working together in us to fulfil our potential in the body of Christ. We need to be filled both with the Spirit and with the Word of God.

See how unbalanced you become when you have one, but not the other. For instance,you may be in a meeting and the Spirit stirs you with the love of God for the people. You have been earnestly desiring to be used in spiritual gifts and as the Spirit rests upon you, you prophesy. It goes something like this: 'My people, I tell you I love you. I love you utterly, through and through, and I love you. My love is fantastic, terrific and wonderful and I love you.'

Now actually there may be someone in great need of that

reassurance, but, for the most part, the people there will know that truth. What will happen is that they will be edified by the heart-felt expression of that truth which they will pick up from your voice. They will recognise in their spirit the Spirit of God stirring you.

The problem is that there will be severe limitations of expression. The Spirit cannot plunge into the reservoir of your mind and stir scriptural thought in you. You will be lame and limited. Often, too, people hold back from stepping out, especially in prophecy, because they fear being shallow. There is an awareness in us that there is not much for the Spirit to work on.

Of course, when you first flex your muscles in spiritual gifts there will be a simplicity and a lack of breadth. Actually, God loves to use simplicity. But as the Word dwells in us richly more and more, so our prophesying will be richer and stronger. Words and phrases start to have hints in them from all over the Scriptures, bringing depth, variety and a richness which encourages, edifies and builds up the whole body of Christ.

When the unction of the Spirit and the power of the Word come together something mighty always happens. Let it be our desire to facilitate that by devoting ourselves to what the Bible has to say.

It develops faith to live by

Here is more evidence of a person whose mind is set on the things of the Spirit. You have faith to live by. The mind set on the Spirit will produce a person who is moving in the dynamics of faith, who is living day by day in the realm of faith. There's a two-stage process to faith as Paul outlines in Romans 10:17. 'Faith comes from hearing the message, and the message is heard through the word of Christ.'

Some folk have funny ideas about faith. Faith is not 'believism'. We do not work ourselves up into a frenzy of 'believism' in an attempt to convince ourselves we have faith. Faith is actually practically the opposite of frenzy. Faith is an inner conviction, an assurance, a deep inner knowing that you have heard from God and are walking with Him.

That is a killer to intellectual pride. Having gone through all the arguments and tested out all the pros and cons we are left with a simple statement: I know because I know.

'What do you mean "because I know"?'

'Because I know that I know.'

Very frustrating for the intellectual approach, but the fruit of a mind set on the Spirit and dwelling on the Word.

Remind yourself of that famous verse on faith, Hebrews 11:1. 'Now faith is being sure of what we hope for and certain of what we do not see.' Faith is being sure. It's not even a risk.

Some people view faith as risk. That is because we exercise faith in the realm of the unseen, the as-yet-to-be-evident. Whether it's about the great truths of Christian doctrine or about a decision in the area of guidance we are talking about an assurance of rightness, not a risk. It may look risky to those who are not exercising faith, but there is no uncertainty in your mind to give rise to any element of risk.

Some people view faith as risk because of the 'stepping out' element. Stepping out requires courage and spiritual strength, but it must be built on an assurance, a certainty, about God and His Word. Faith is not believism or presumption.

Neither is it a magical formula. God is not restricted to our rules and He will often surprise us and challenge us in the way things happen. He doesn't want a lot of automata following their noses through sets of rules. He wants a vibrant, daily relationship full of life and variety.

Our problems with faith lie in our minds. It's often a battle in the mind. For example, if someone asks for prayer for healing, the first thought is, 'Great! An opportunity to see God do something here.' My second thought is a doubt that anything will happen. Why? Usually because:

1. I'm cynical – renew the mind.
2. I've prayed for people in the past and nothing's happened – renew the mind with the promises of God.
3. I'm not sure the person himself/herself even believes anything will happen – renew the mind. It's up to God, not them.
4. The enemy himself doesn't want me to be effective and is flying in with the temptation to disbelieve God – renew the mind.

Martyn Lloyd-Jones has emphasised a very helpful phrase: *doubt is faith under pressure*. Doubt is faith in a battle, a bit of a crisis if you like. Doubt is not unbelief. It is belief under challenge. Lloyd-Jones went on to make another helpful statement: *doubt comes when I listen to myself rather than speak truth to myself.*

If I speak the truth of the Word of God to myself, if I proclaim His promises and His character, I am encouraging the faith I already have. I am doing the opposite to allowing the doubts to dominate. I challenge doubts with the Word.

This isn't 'believism' because faith is already there. The point is that the renewed mind, the disciplined mind, the soaked-in-the-Word mind will encourage that faith into strength and action. The unrenewed mind simply wallows in doubt and indecision.

2. Be a worshipper

A second way of improving your thinking is to nurture your renewed mind by being a worshipper. Jesus reminded us of the basis of the Ten Commandments in Matthew 22:37. A feature is that we are to love the Lord 'with all our mind'.

Paul knew what it was to have a worshipping mind. In 1 Corinthians 14:14,15 he tells us that his practice includes singing and praying with his mind. He doesn't want his mind to be unfruitful in a worship context. Being a daily worshipper improves your mind. It brings clarity, perception and balance.

3. Be of one mind

Your thinking is improved when you are not in isolation, but in fellowship with others. Submitting our thinking to one another requires humility and effort on our part when it would be easier to go it alone.

Paul says, 'Stand firm in one spirit, contending as one man

for the faith of the gospel . . . being one in spirit and purpose' (Phil 1:27; 2:2). What does this mean in reality? Does it mean you don't have opinions? Does it mean you lose your individuality? No, of course not. None of these 'scare stories' is true to real inter-relationship and commitment.

The key to it all is that we keep our individuality, those marks of personality that are as precious to God as to us. What we lose is our independence – which is actually a curse to growth and maturity in the body of Christ. It's interesting to note that one of the marks of a cult is that people lose their individuality as well as their independence. Of course, we want to avoid cultism, but let us not throw out the baby with the bathwater! It is God's command that we learn to submit our thinking to one another.

I have a calling on my life to be of one mind with my brothers and sisters. It's nothing to do with committing intellectual suicide or becoming empty in my thinking. It has everything to do with adding in my gifts and my distinctive qualities to help build the life of the church, and letting others knock the edges off me.

Submit yourselves to one another and your thinking will be improved – there is no doubt about that. Elsewhere (Eph 4) Paul calls us to maintain the unity of the Spirit until we attain the unity of the faith. We are all seeking to be better representatives of Christ, aren't we? You are not the only one with that goal in mind. Take hold of humility and grasp the opportunity of being of one mind.

10. And Finally – Winning Minds

I love most sports and really enjoy them, but if there's one sport I cannot stand it's cross-country running. When I was in my first year at senior school we had compulsory trials for the cross-country team. You can probably remember this experience yourself – most games masters and mistresses seem to have devised their own form of purgatory along similar lines. The first twenty would be in the team, and, just to make it interesting, the last twenty would do it all again.

'No problem,' I thought. 'At least twenty in front, at least twenty behind, easy!' Off we set. I kept a big pack ahead of me and a big pack behind. No problem. We crossed the finishing line, and, to my horror, number nineteen was yours truly! Maths never was my strong point.

For a whole year I ran in that team. I didn't care whether we won or lost. I learned every trick in the book to avoid actually running, from feigned stitch to hiding in the sweet shop for a couple of laps. I had no motivation, no determination, no desire to win. My mind had backed out before we even started.

Some of the boys were good. They were in with a chance every time. They would push through barriers of real stitch, pass by the temptation of slipping into the sweet shop. They wanted to give it their best; they wanted to run and they had the winning mentality. I just didn't have the winning mentality. I was a pushover and a loser.

Paul says, 'Run in such a way as to get the prize' (1 Cor 9:24). Later on (verse 26) Paul adds emphasis by saying, 'I do not run like a man running aimlessly.' My aim is to see my mind renewed. I know it's possible, I know I can win, and I am determined to do so. I'm not going to simply roll along through life aimlessly. I want the prize!

If I am going to run a winning race I must have this mentality. It is crucial if I am actually going to see change in my thinking and my life.

Clear vision

Hebrews 12:1,2 also tells us that in this race I need to throw off every hindrance to effective running. I need to run with perseverance and I need to keep my eyes fixed on Jesus. I will never have a winning mentality if I'm not clear in my thinking. There is so much confusion around today in the area of the mind, much of it no longer rooted in intellectualism, but in a new form of 'spirituality'. People call it 'New Age', but New Age is very difficult to define because it is so subtle and indeed has managed to permeate almost every aspect of modern life from the obvious to the hidden.

If I am to win, then my mind must become uncluttered. I must have 'clear vision'. I need discernment today, like never before. I need to be on my toes, be well informed and have my eyes wide open. It's not that we become paranoid about everything we see and hear, but we would do well to find out about the philosophies behind much modern thinking today. We are, after all, to be very much in the world while at the same time not being of it! How often evangelicalism has translated that prayer of Jesus for us (Jn 17) in an outward mode – how you dress, where you visit, who you are seen with. As the years have gone by I have been increasingly convinced that it really has to do with that which is within. Your heart attitude and most certainly your thought patterns.

It really is time for a new generation of Christians to emerge who are clear in this thinking – no longer hindered by legalistic shackles, and no longer hoodwinked by 'New Age' spirituality. A generation transformed by the renewing of their minds and therefore not conformed to the pattern of this world, but rather changing their world to the glory of God.

This book has taken you behind the scenes, as it were, into the backdrop to the battle of your mind. We have looked at the state your mind was in before you came to Christ and the ways in which the process of renewal takes place. We have looked at the enemy's only weapon and the way he uses it on the battlefield. We have seen how to deal with him and counterattack, and how to build a new mind set on the things of the Spirit, full of the Word of God.

Now, go for it! You have the capacity; the power at work within you is more than sufficient. Will you take up the challenge to be transformed by the renewing of your mind? Will you be a winner?

PART THREE

Study Guide

1. How Vital Is the Renewed Mind?

1. What was your first reaction on reading the title of this book?
2. The writer recalls a personal example of temptation leading to a thought, leading to an action. Can you come up with any examples from your own experience?
3. In your first years as a believer, what changes were you aware of in your thinking? Were these gradual or immediate?
4. How did your new mind-set affect the way you acted? What adjustments in your lifestyle did this lead to?
5. If you now consider that God is involved in your life, giving it meaning, purpose and direction, how does this compare with the way you used to think?
6. Look again at this list of symptoms of the uncontrolled mind at work (stress and anxiety, sexual temptation, cynicism, negativism, self-pity, anger, fears). If 'God's ultimate purpose is for us all to become like Jesus', what did Jesus model in each of these areas of His life?

2. The State of Your Mind

1. 'Without Christ your mind is darkened and your thinking is futile.' How do you feel about a statement like this? Would you have reacted differently a few years ago?
2. What major issues of the day (on the national and international scene) indicate that man's conscience is in a muddle?
3. If there was a moment in your life when God 'lifted the veil' so that you began to understand biblical truth, describe how it came about.
4. What *practical* difference has it made to you that you have been cleansed from a guilty conscience by the blood of Jesus?
5. If you still struggle with the same weaknesses and problems after becoming a Christian, how might this make you feel?
6. Why should understanding that permanent change is *gradual* rather than *instant* be releasing for us?

3. Who Do You Think You Are?

1. What good values were instilled in you in childhood?
2. Are you aware of any negative words or incidents from your childhood which began to shape the way you thought about yourself?
3. How does it make you feel if you are always struggling to meet someone else's expectations?
4. Share some personal stories of the way God has set you free from negative influences or traumatic events in your life.
5. What messages come across in the most popular television 'soaps'?
6. As a Christian, what specific cultural clashes do you come across in your school, college, work, or among your circle of friends? How do you think Jesus would handle these?

4. Taking Every Thought Captive

1. In what ways are you aware of there being a battle for your mind?
2. Do you have personal examples of the way an enemy stronghold can remain in your thought life even after you belong to Christ?
3. If you have experienced God's power to free you from the grip of some stronghold, share it for the benefit of those who may be struggling with something at the moment.
4. Were you able to identify with the description of the enemy suddenly zooming into your thought life in destructive ways? What practical steps can we take to keep any vulnerable 'landing strips' off-limits for the enemy of our souls?
5. What are the telltale signs of becoming lazy and ill-disciplined in our thinking? As members of the body of Christ, how can we help each other?
6. Look at Matthew 4:1–11. How did Jesus handle temptation when the devil flung it at Him? What can you find in this passage to instruct and encourage you?

5. Replacement, Not Removal!

1. 'Fill your mind with right thoughts and the wrong thoughts go.' Sounds simple – but what challenges are you likely to face?
2. How do you feel about the familiar saying that someone is 'too heavenly minded to be of any earthly use'? How does Jesus measure up to this statement?
3. What new 'righteous ruts' of thinking did you have to concentrate on *first* as a new believer? What are the issues that you need to give special attention to *now*?
4. How do you go about reading your Bible and meditating on Scripture? What fresh impetus might be helpful for you? What have you learned along the way that might help someone else?
5. Are there particular biblical truths that you find it difficult to agree with? What are they? Why do you think you have a struggle with them?
6. Share any personal experience of being set free from fear through a Bible truth.

6. The Sword – Expose the Root

1. God's Word in the Bible is 'not for display purposes, to be hung on a wall and gazed at'. What do you think this means, and is it a danger for us?
2. Can you recall any decisive moments in your life when God's Word spoke right into your life, exposing a root issue?
3. What has God shown you about yourself or said to you through your reading of Scripture in recent weeks?
4. What could you do to counteract passivity and stimulate more passion for God?
5. How can we help each other as members of the body of Christ to attack these root issues of pride, lack of faith, and lack of devotion – through the Word of God?
6. Read the description of Jesus appearing in His glory to the apostle John, in Revelation 1:9–18. What do you understand by verse 16, 'out of his mouth came a sharp double-edged sword'? How does this make you feel as far as your relationship to Jesus is concerned?

7. The Sword – Expose the Enemy

1. Have you made it a practice to memorise Scripture verses? What might be the value of this in the battle for the mind?
2. What down-to-earth difference does it make to you to know that you are now 'in Christ'?
3. You still face sin's lure (and sometimes fall to it), but what difference is there in your attitude to sin and temptation now, compared to before you knew Jesus?
4. Of what comfort and encouragement is it to know that Christ was tempted like you, and way beyond you – yet without sinning?
5. What encouragement can you find in 1 Corinthians 10:13?
6. Are you aware of particular times and situations when you are especially assaulted by temptation? What have you learned to do about it?

8. Improving Your Thinking

1. Consider the newspapers and magazines that are read in your home; the radio station that you play most of the time; how much television you watch; the computer games you or your children play. Talk together about how our thinking might be affected by these and other daily influences.
2. In what ways have you become a more creative or accomplished person since turning to Christ? Encourage one another by pointing to the progress different members of the group have made.
3. Do you review your life periodically and set personal or family goals? What new challenges have you taken on in recent years?
4. Is there something you have dreamt of doing but pushed to the back of your mind?
5. How can we help each other to press through mistakes and failure?
6. Are you aware of God's Spirit stretching or stirring you in some new way at this stage of your Christian growth?

9. Mind Your Mind

1. How important is the way you start the day? What challenges do you personally have to handle in order to begin your day with a godly mind-set?
2. God's verdict on you is more important than how you feel about yourself. As a group see how many positive truths you can recall from Scripture that speak of how God views us now that we are 'in Christ'.
3. Are you ready and able to get alongside a new believer to help equip them for their life in Christ? If not, in what areas do you think you need help to make progress first?
4. What do you find stimulates you to worship God with all your mind?
5. How can we develop our worship when we meet together, so that we enjoy the glory of Christ, and our guests realise that God is real and present?
6. How can we avoid the extremes of being independent on the one hand, or ending up as clones on the other?

10. And Finally – Winning Minds

1. How has this book helped you to have more of a winning mentality?
2. What specific adjustments have you already made as a result of understanding the importance of the renewed mind? Are there others you still need to make?
3. Have you begun to win any new victories in your battle for the mind? Name them, and encourage one another.
4. How can we help others, in our circle of friends and family, in their battle for the mind?